Praise for *The Joy of Getting It Done:*

One of the most frustrating things about human nature is our resistance to positive change. We know what we should do but we don't do it. Linda King's 10 tools are genius for getting around our stumbling blocks. Inspiring and often humorous, Linda gives us simple, step-by-step guidance to make our lives go the way we want.

—Judy Robbins, Psy.D., psychotherapist

The Joy of Getting It Done teaches the productivity tools and insights that are essential to students' success in school, especially those students who suffer from ADD or ADHD. Linda King's 10 tools will put students in a better position to manage their time effectively and improve the quality of their educational experience. I personally used her techniques to finish the writing of a book within six months, having procrastinated on its completion for over seven years. This book will help any conscientious student to compete in an increasingly global environment.

Dr. Ernest M. Marino, author,
Ahead: How to Make the Most of Your College Experience

Linda King has put together a book that will change your life. She has succinct, approachable and very concrete tips for getting things done. And they work! Her 10 tools are well-crafted and accompanied by worksheets that you will want to use over and over. You will build new, productive habits and Linda has even included tips for what to do if you run out of steam or fall back into old habits. This is a book that will help everyone who reads it – not just those with ADHD. If you follow her sound advice, you'll be amazed at the way you will get things done!

—Martha Hennessey, Ph.D., Licensed Clinical Mental
Health Counselor, Board Certified Coach

the Joy of Getting It DONE

10 TOOLS TO HELP YOU STOP WASTING TIME AND START MANAGING IT

Linda King, ACC, AACC

Linwal Press

Thanks to Alain Riazuelo, IAP/UPMC/CNRS, for use of the black hole image on page 76.

Published by Linwal Press
Printed in the United States of America

ISBN-13: 978-0-9911069-0-5

Acknowledgments

I'd like to express my heartfelt gratitude for those people who have supported me personally and professionally. Without them, I could never have created this book.

First, many thanks to my clients. I learn from each of you every time we speak.

Thanks to Annie Duvall, my editor extraordinaire, who smoothed out my language and always offered good suggestions.

I'm grateful for Keri Adams-Gagne's excellent graphic design work as she patiently incorporated many rounds of changes into the final book cover and title page.

Thanks to Kathleen M. Victory Hannisian of Blue Pencil Consulting for her wonderful consultative feedback and her logistical help with the publishing process.

Much appreciation to my friends Judy and Emily, who allowed me photographic rights to their closet.

Many thanks to my dear friend Mimi, who always encouraged me to become a life coach and ADHD coach, and ultimately named my practice.

Much gratitude to my children Eric and Suzie. You keep me humble! Raising you has been the most profound experience of my life. I couldn't be more proud of both of you.

Above all, thanks to my beloved husband, Walt Tuvell, for supporting me every step of the way. You are always there for me as my technical guru when I am cursing the computer. You never let me forget how much you believe in and value me. I am happy to share this life with you.

With appreciation,
Linda King

Table of Contents

Welcome..1

Part 1 – Getting Started

Laying Out Your Goals...5
New Routines...6
Tasks You Avoid...8
Tackling an Overwhelming Project...10
The Stage Is Set..12

Part 2 – The 10 Tools

Tool #1: Use a Whole Number..15
Creating a New Routine..16
Using Whole Numbers for Tasks You Avoid..16
Tackling an Overwhelming Project...17
Limiting an Activity...18
Summary...19
Exercises..20

Tool #2: Start Small and Increase Slowly...24
Consider a Different Approach..25
More Ways to Apply Tool #2...27
Summary...27
Exercise..27

Tool #3: Break It Down into Manageable Pieces..............................29
The Typical Approach...29
Divide and Conquer..30
Tackling Other Big Jobs..31
Summary...32
Exercises..33

Tool #4: Make Your Decision Ahead of Time...................................35
The Overeaters Anonymous Approach..35
Planning Ahead..36
Summary...37
Exercises..38

Tool #5: Make It a Commitment..41

Make a Public Declaration..42
Do It Despite Adversity...42
Have a Contingency Plan...43
Is It Ever Okay Just to Try without Actually Committing?...........43
Are You Ready?..44
Summary..44
Exercises...44

Tool #6: Make It Part of an Existing Routine...................55

Doing It at the Same Time Every Day......................................55
Doing It before or after a Specific Activity...............................56
"Binding" the New Routine to an Established Routine.................57
Summary..58
Exercises...59

Tool #7: Deal with Distractions...61

Reaching Your Goal..63
Distracting People...63
Summary..64
Exercises...64

Tool #8: Reward Yourself..69

Premack's Principle..69
Big Ticket Rewards...71
Additional Motivation..72
Summary..72
Exercises...72

Tool #9: Avoid Your Personal Black Holes........................76

What Sucks You In?..76
Are You Enjoying or Avoiding?...76
Summary..77
Exercise...78

Tool #10: Get Support...80

Get Support by Announcing Your Intentions.............................80
Find a Buddy...81
Support Groups..81
Who Are Your Support People?...82
Hiring a Coach...83
Summary..83
Exercises...84

Part 3 – Putting It All Together

Creating the Plan...**91**
New Routines...91
Tasks You Avoid..93
Overwhelming Projects..95
But What If...97

Part 4 – Staying on Course

Maintaining Change...**101**
Decrease the Amount..101
Get Support..101
Was the Change Right for You?..102
Is It Maintainable?...102
Right Change, Wrong Implementation?.......................................102
Call In the Pros..103

Overcoming Obstacles...**104**
Not Ready to Change..104
Boundary Issues..105
Not Knowing Your Own Style...105
Facing the Feelings..106

Acquiring Stuff...**107**

Parting Thoughts..**109**

Appendix – The Questionnaires

Looking at Your Life..**113**
Your Personal Time..114
Your Personal Stuff and Space..118
Your Personal Information Management.......................................122
Your Life Logistics..126
Your Personal Wellness...130
Your Personal Finances...136
Your Professional Time..140
Your Professional Stuff and Space..147
Your Professional Information Management................................150

Endnotes..**155**

Welcome

As a life coach and ADHD coach, I help my clients work on the challenges they face with time management and organization. You don't have to have a formal diagnosis of ADHD* to be struggling with some of its challenges. If you're like me and most of my clients, you probably have at least a little ADHD in a few areas of your life. This book is about the 10 *Joy of Getting It Done* tools that can help you overcome those challenges, get more organized and use your time more effectively.

The information in this book was originally developed as a presentation that I give to community and professional groups. I tried to lay out the pages in a way that would give the feel of attending one of my talks, with lots of pictures and easy-to-read text. When you are already overwhelmed, the information you need to get control of your time should slide down easily.

For many, the best way to approach this program is to work through it a little at a time. You can do a chapter a day, a chapter a week or even a chapter a month, but whatever frequency you choose, do it on a regular schedule and always mark the next session on your calendar before you quit the current one.

You might find it helpful to work through this program with a few other people. You can bounce ideas off of each other, provide support and help each other come up with ways to apply the tools. Meeting regularly will motivate you to stay on track and see it through.

Working through this program is a journey, not a sprint. Don't be tempted to rush into the next chapter until you've absorbed the material from the current one.

You'll probably want to start making changes right away and apply each new technique as soon as it's presented. That's fine, but if you hit a rough patch, I'd suggest that you try again after you complete the program so you have the whole picture when you set up your plan.

---

* I use "ADHD" to refer to both Attention Deficit and Hyperactivity Disorder and Attention Deficit Disorder (ADD).

If you like to write, or if you keep a journal, consider writing down your thoughts and feelings as you work your way through the program. Coaches often encourage their clients to explore their feelings as they make changes, becoming aware of resistance and other feelings that might be holding them back.

If you find that you are really stuck and unable to make effective change on your own, you might want to consider seeking the services of a life coach, ADHD coach or other helping professional. We'll explore how to find one in *Tool #10: Get Support*.

I personally have found *The Joy of Getting It Done* tools to be life-changing, as have many of my clients and the people who attend my presentations. As someone who has her own time challenges, I speak from experience. There is not a single tool in this program that I have not used, and continue to use. Throughout the book, I give many examples of how I've used the tools in my own life. I also give examples of how clients and *Joy of Getting It Done* workshop participants have used them. In those cases, I've changed the names and other personal details to ensure confidentiality.

As you go through the program, feel free to share your thoughts on my blog, *www.JoyofGTD.com/blog*, or my *Joy of Getting Things Done* Facebook page, *www.facebook.com/JoyofGTD*.

Now, it's time to set some goals.

Part 1
Getting Started

Laying Out Your Goals

Before you start *The Joy of Getting It Done* program, it will be useful for you to have some specific goals in mind. That way, you can apply what you are learning and get practice using the tools.

You might find the questionnaires in the Appendix helpful in quantifying and solidifying some of your objectives.

Be sure to make your goals "SMART." They should be:

Specific – What exactly are you planning to achieve? ("Exercise regularly," not "Live a healthier lifestyle" – too vague)

Measurable – How much will you do? ("I'll exercise 30 minutes/day.")

Action-oriented – What action are you going to take? ("Work out on the cardio machines at the Y")

Realistic – Is it realistic for *you*?

Timely – When are you going to do it? ("I'll go to the Y each weekday morning before work.")

Throughout the program, exercises in each chapter will help you figure out exactly how to apply the tools so that you can achieve your objectives. But first let's set some up. We're specifically going to look at three different types of goals as we go through the program:

- Incorporating new routines into your life
- Creating a new approach to tasks you avoid
- Tackling overwhelming projects

As you lay out your goals, I'll ask you to consider how it feels to have them in their current state, and then I'll ask you to imagine how it might feel to have achieved them. It's important to jot down at least a few thoughts and feelings so that if you find that you are flagging a bit, you can look back and get a new shot of motivation. Let's get started.

New Routines

What new routines would you like to introduce into your life? Name up to three, then prioritize them 1, 2 and 3 in order of your motivation to get started on them. Assign a one-word label to each routine that you'll use to refer to it as you go through the book.

New Routine	Priority	Label

What are some of the feelings that come to mind with not having these routines as part of your life? Examples might be "out of control," "unhealthy" or "anxious."

Routine (Label)	Feelings Associated with Not Having This Routine

Who else, if anyone, is affected by your not having these routines established?

Routine	Others Affected by Your Not Having This Routine in Your Life

Close your eyes and imagine that each of these routines has become a regular part of your life. For each one, write some feelings that come to mind as a result of establishing this routine. Examples might be "peaceful," "empowered" and "on top of things."

Routine	Feelings Associated with Establishing This Routine

As you work through the program, pick only *one* of these routines to introduce into your life, probably the one you decided was your number one priority. Once the first routine is firmly established in your life – for a period of at least 6 months or even a year – you can introduce the next one.

Tasks You Avoid

One of the topics addressed in this program is making better use of the time you spend working on things. You'll find ideas for better focusing, minimizing distractions and staying on task, and overcoming procrastination.

Pick three tasks that you need to do regularly but that you tend to avoid doing. Usually they are items that are boring, repetitive or not pleasant, but unfortunately must be done. This time don't prioritize them, just choose a label for each one.

Task Description	Label

How do you feel when you are working on these tasks?

Task	Feelings Associated with Working on This Task

Who else, if anyone, is adversely affected by your avoiding these tasks?

Task	Others Affected by Your Avoiding This Task

When you do complete these tasks, how does it feel?

Task	Feelings Associated with Completing This Task

You can work on any or all of these tasks as you go through the program.

Tackling an Overwhelming Project

What major projects do you need to address? Name up to three, then prioritize them 1, 2 and 3 in order from most important to least important. Assign a one-word label to each project that you'll use to refer to it as you go through the program.

Priority	Overwhelming Project Description	Label

What are some of the feelings that you associate with having each of these projects hanging over your head?

Project	Feelings Associated with This Project Being Unfinished

Who else, if anyone, is adversely affected by these projects not being done?

Project	Others Affected by Its Incompletion

Now imagine that each project is done. For each one, write some feelings that come to mind as a result of having it off of your plate.

Project	Feelings Associated with Completing This Project

Choose one, two or three projects you want to work on as you go through the book. Sometimes rotating through them helps keep interest up, especially if they are significantly different, like cleaning out a closet vs. doing your taxes. Or, you might prefer to get through them one at a time. Either approach can work.

The Stage Is Set

By now you should have decided upon one new routine to introduce into your life and you should have chosen at least one big project to work on. Hopefully, you've also thought about the tasks that you must regularly do that you tend to avoid or struggle to stay focused on when you are doing them. The exercises throughout the book will help you figure out strategies to get them done.

In the next chapter, you'll start learning the simple and practical tools that will help you achieve your goals.

If you've really spent some time thoughtfully filling out these exercises, it might be good to stop for now and start on Part 2 when you are fresh. But do one more thing before you go – decide exactly *when* you are going to work on the next section and *mark it on your calendar*. You'll have a far better chance of getting back to the program if you set a date and time for the next session than if you plan to do it whenever you get around to it.

Part 2
The 10 Tools

Tool #1:
Use a Whole Number

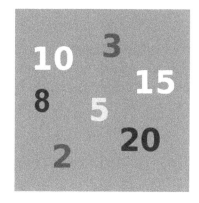

Any time you set out to accomplish something, decide how much you want to achieve in each session. Use whole numbers to set up goals for yourself, for example: I'm going to pay 5 bills; or I'm going to declutter for 15 minutes; or I'm going to read 3 pages of that chapter that I'm dreading reading. When you decide on a specific amount that you are going to do, it makes the task closed-ended, which is less overwhelming. You can pick a number – no matter how small – that you feel comfortable doing. That way, you set yourself up for success and that's very motivating!

Sometimes, the easiest way to assign a whole number to an activity is to set a simple kitchen timer for a specific number of minutes. If you are procrastinating, the timer can help you get going by making the activity time-limited. Setting your timer for a specific amount of time can make the activity feel less daunting. Even if it is something distasteful that you hate, you know that the timer will go off and you can stop. "I'm going to update my résumé" can feel overwhelming. "I'm going to spend 20 minutes working on my résumé" can feel doable.

You don't have to use a timer. You can use any unit, like writing 2 pages of a report or entering 10 clients into a database. The point is to set an objective that is *specific and measurable.* It makes your goal SMART.

When you get to your goal, you can quit for now, knowing you have reached your objective for today. Or, if you feel like it, you can set another goal and keep going. There are times that I spend several hours on a project by working in 20-minute chunks and continually resetting the timer. Having a time-limited goal makes it easier to get started. Knowing that I can quit when the timer goes off keeps me productive. Sometimes I get so involved in my task that when the timer beeps, I just turn it off and keep going.

Creating a New Routine

Using whole numbers can help you introduce new routines into your life, like:

- Walking 30 minutes 5 times a week; or
- Following up with 3 clients each morning; or
- Processing half an inch of paper each evening.

Remember, when you set an objective, it's really important to pick an amount that's palatable to you. *If you find that you're avoiding doing something, you've probably planned to do more than you're comfortable doing,* so scale it back.

Using Whole Numbers for Tasks You Avoid

When you use whole numbers to set a goal, it helps you focus on the task at hand even when you don't enjoy it because you know there's an end in sight.

Decide On How Much to Do in One Sitting

Once again (and I can't say it enough), pick a number or an amount that is doable and not daunting. There's a much better chance you'll start, instead of procrastinating, if you're not overwhelmed by the amount you're planning to do.

No Interruptions until Finished

Once you get started, vow not to let anything distract you. Instead, focus completely on the task. Don't check email, don't answer the phone, don't stop to get a cup of coffee. Those things that are trying to distract you will still be there when you get done.

Visualize a Barrier

Before you start, think of some sort of imaginary barrier that will remain in place until you're done. For example, if you are working at your desk, think about how your body feels where it contacts the chair, and imagine that this contact can't be broken until you get to your goal.

Example: *The Joy of Getting Things Done* Newsletter

When I sit down to start writing my monthly newsletter, it can be quite intimidating to stare at a blank page. I'm tempted to let anything distract me. But setting the timer for 20 minutes, and knowing that I can quit when it beeps, both gets me going and keeps me focused.

Usually by the time an uninterrupted 20 minutes is up, I'm tooling along and I continue writing until I've finished the first draft. But if the timer goes off and the words just aren't flowing, I'll call it quits and try again tomorrow.

Tackling an Overwhelming Project

Using a whole number for tackling a large job is really effective at taking the overwhelm out of it. Again, the most important thing is to decide on an amount that is not intimidating. There are some tasks that are just so onerous that working on them for just 20 minutes is too much; in fact even 10 minutes can feel like too much.

In those cases, it's fine to work away at a project for just five or three or if it's really awful, even one minute at a time. Obviously you won't get much done, but at least you'll be making some forward motion. Choosing a tiny goal can help you feel less anxious about the project. It often happens that when you're working on a project for just a couple of minutes at a time, you start to realize that it's not as bad as you thought it was. Then you can start doing larger chunks.

Example 1: Cleaning Out the Attic

My attic had done what attics tend to do – that is, become full of stuff. Every time I thought about cleaning it out, I just couldn't face it, so I procrastinated. Well, one Saturday I decided to take my own advice. I set the timer for 20 minutes and got to work. When the timer went off, I was surprised at the dent I'd made!

My timer and I continued to work on the attic almost every weekend. When it went off, I either stopped for the day or I set it again. Occasionally, when it went off, I put it away and finished up the section I was working on. But mostly when I wanted to keep going, I kept resetting the timer. The project just felt too big not to have that crutch. It took several months, but I got it cleaned out.

Example 2: Weeding the Garden

Here's an example of a different way of using whole numbers. We have a large garden in our yard, and in the spring, the weeds can take over. If I just go out and start weeding I end up feeling that it's hopeless. Then when I get tired, I don't have much sense of satisfaction since all I can see are the parts that I didn't get to. So instead, I mentally choose a 10-12 square foot area and concentrate on that. It's a very manageable amount, and when I'm finished, I can look at that weed-free area and feel a lot of satisfaction. Then if I'm up for it, I can do another section.

You can get quite creative in finding ways to use whole numbers to help you get things done. Beverly spent some time each weekend cleaning out a room. She'd put on a favorite music CD and get to work. When the CD was done, so was she!

Limiting an Activity

You can also use a whole number to limit activities that you tend to spend too much time on.

Taking Breaks

When you're working on something that's intense or tiring, it's important to take breaks. However, it can be easy to get distracted during a break, especially if the job is something you don't particularly enjoy doing. By setting a timer to limit the break, you can keep it from expanding into wasted time.

Losing Yourself

Most of us have activities that we need to do, but that suck us in. Before we know it, hours have gone by.

Take email for example. We all have to check it occasionally, but if we're not careful, we can waste a lot of time reading and passing along those funny emails that people send, or clicking on links that we don't even care about. Beatrice had this problem until she started setting the timer. That made her focus on the important emails and skip the time wasters.

Taking Too Long on a Task

Sometimes it's easy to spend more time on a task than it really deserves. Setting a timer to limit the time you spend on it can help you work quickly and efficiently without getting bogged down with unimportant details.

Make It a Race

Finally, using the timer to make a task into a race can turn an otherwise boring activity into something that can actually be kind of fun. Now maybe I have a low standard for what fun is, but for those of us with a little bit – or even a lot – of ADHD, racing against the timer can provide just enough stimulation to make a task that is deadly dull more interesting.

Summary

Using a whole number, either in the form of a number of minutes or as a specific number of units to do (e.g. 3 pages), can make a task or routine you are avoiding a lot easier to face. It can make your goals SMART. Always pick a number that feels comfortable to do, no matter how small. If you start feeling resistance, scale back.

You can also use whole numbers to limit an activity that you tend to get lost in or that you generally spend too much time doing. If you set a timer, then find that you hit the "off" button subconsciously when it buzzes, set it far enough away that you have to get up to turn it off.

Exercises

New Routines

For each of the routines you identified as a goal (p. 6), how could you break it down into a whole number? Some examples – number of pieces accomplished, a specific space or area, a distance or a specific amount of time.

Routine	Whole Number Goal

Tasks You Avoid

How could you break down the tasks that you regularly avoid (p. 8) into a whole number?

Task	Whole Number Goal

Overwhelming Projects

Think of the projects you identified (p. 10) and assign a whole number goal to each one.

Project	Whole Number Goal

Limiting Activities

The following questions are designed to make you more aware of how you may be wasting time, and help you use whole numbers to come up with a plan to use your time better.

Taking breaks:

1. Do you find that after working intensely for a while, you need to take a break?

   ___ Yes   ___ No (skip to "Losing Yourself")   ___ Occasionally

2. Which statement is most accurate for you?
   ___ I take a brief break, then get back to work (skip to "Losing Yourself").
   ___ I plan to take a brief break, but it always ends up being longer.

3. How many minutes would you consider to be an appropriate amount for a break?
   ___ 5 minutes
   ___ 10 minutes
   ___ 15 minutes
   ___ 20+ minutes

Losing Yourself

In the first column, name up to three activities that you need to do but that suck you in (email, internet, etc.).

In the second column, map out a specific plan for limiting those activities when you find that you are wasting time with them.

Activity	How will you limit it?

Tasks That Take Too Long

In the first column, identify up to three tasks that you often spend too much time completing.

In the second column, write the amount of time that you often spend on these tasks.

In the third column, write down an amount of time that would be more appropriate for each of these tasks.

Task	How much time do you usually spend doing it?	How much time would be appropriate to spend on it?

Racing with the Timer

Name some tasks that are boring that might be a little more interesting in a race with a timer, then write the number of minutes you could set on the timer when you do this task.

Task	Timer Setting

In the next chapter, we'll explore how starting with a small change and increasing slowly can be the most effective way to succeed for the long haul.

If you are stopping now, write down the date and time of your next session on the calendar.

Tool #2:
Start Small and Increase Slowly

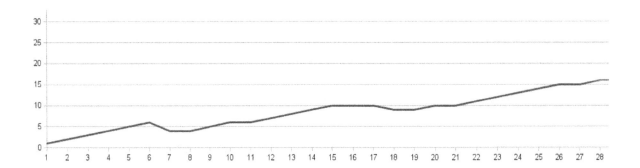

How often have you tried to establish a new routine in your life, such as exercising or eating better, only to fail after a week or two? Often the problem comes from diving in hook, line and sinker at the very beginning. Adrenaline and enthusiasm can get you going, but when they fade out, so do you.

For instance, sometimes people decide that they are going to get in shape all at once, so the first day they spend an hour lifting weights at the gym or they try to run a mile.

The second day, they don't do it again because they can't move, or they are in the coronary care unit of the local hospital. They decide that getting in shape is just too hard right now. Sigh. Maybe next year...

Consider a Different Approach

For many, the secret to incorporating a new habit is starting small and building gradually:

- Make one small change.
- Do it until it becomes a habit.
- Add a little to it.

Example 1: Walking

Research has shown the many benefits of regular walking. We know that in order to get the full benefit of walking, you need to do it at least 30 minutes several times a week. But if you are a couch potato, or just completely out of the routine of regular exercise, 30 minutes can seem like a very, very long time indeed.

But what if you started out with a very small amount, maybe even just one minute a day? Does that seem overwhelming? And what if you did that one minute a day every day for a week? That's a pretty non-intimidating amount for even the couchiest of couch potatoes among us.

Now no one thinks that a one-minute daily walk is going to deliver many health benefits, but what if the next week you walked 2 minutes each day? Then, the next week you walked 3 minutes each day, and the week after that you walked 4 minutes each day? If you continued to build up one minute a day each week, at the end of 30 weeks, you'd be walking your 30 minutes.

That change did not happen fast; it took about 7 months to achieve. But by the end of those 7 months, it has become a regular part of your life. Had you started doing all 30 minutes a day right out of the gate, there is a good chance that sometime during those 7 months, you would have quit.

You don't have to increase one minute per week. You could increase even more slowly, holding at one amount for a few weeks before adding any more minutes. What's important is that you increase in increments that you can comfortably tolerate. So what if it takes a year to get to 30 minutes? Isn't that better, at the end of that year, than not having done it at all?

This starting small approach isn't about building up physical endurance; most people have the ability to begin a walking program that starts out at more than one minute a day. What

I'm talking about is building up "psychological endurance" – which is, after all, what Starting Small and Increasing Slowly is all about.

Of course any time you want to start a new exercise routine, you should always check with your doctor.

Example 2: Healthier Eating

Back in 2008, I realized that I was eating too much processed and junk food, and it was starting to catch up with me in the form of some health issues. I decided it was time to overhaul my eating habits, and I read a book that promised a relatively simple approach to eating well.

The book was an easy read and provided a lot of good information, but by the end of it I was completely overwhelmed. It just felt hopeless and I threw up my hands. But later, I decided that although I couldn't revamp my entire diet overnight, I could make one change, like introducing one healthier food into my breakfast. Once that became a habit, I introduced another one, and another one until my breakfast consisted of all healthy, non-processed foods. Then I started working on my lunch.

It took me a full year to change my diet, but I've been eating well ever since and I've never reverted to my old eating habits. Sometimes I backslide a bit, and occasionally I eat some junk food, but mostly my eating habits are significantly improved from what they used to be.

Example 3: Strength Training

I'm the original 98-pound weakling. I'm not particularly strong by nature, plus I never had any interest in strength training. However, five years ago a bone scan, combined with reports of how we start to lose muscle mass after 40, convinced me it was time to consider lifting weights. I started off at home on my own with free weights, built up too quickly, and ended up with a serious case of tendinitis.

Several weeks of physical therapy later, I decided to try it again, this time using the strength machines at my local YMCA. Each machine has a computerized screen so I could see how many pounds I lifted and how many repetitions I did on the previous workout, making it much easier to keep track of increasing slowly.

I started out significantly under my weight-lifting ability and just did six machines. I went faithfully three times a week, but I was lifting such small weight amounts and increasing so slowly that I didn't see much strength benefit for a very long time. But the workouts were really easy to do, so I didn't feel much resistance (no pun intended) to going. What I did get, however, was an excellent habit of doing regular strength training – and I stayed injury-free. I eventually added in more machines. By the time I got to the point where I was working hard and gaining real strength, the workouts had become a part of my life. It took well over a year – probably closer to two years! – for me to get to that point. Today, I still don't particularly enjoy strength training workouts, but it's no longer a decision to go. I just do it. I feel very good about doing them, and I can actually see improvements in my strength in my day-to-day life.

More Ways to Apply Tool #2

What if you started tackling that paper backlog on your desk for three minutes per day? If you're not good at returning phone calls, could you start by doing just one a day, first thing in the morning?

Overwhelmed by clutter? Try cleaning off one small surface, maybe just an end table or your nightstand, and keep it absolutely clutter-free for a month. Then choose another surface, and keep it and the original surface clean.

Summary

By Starting Small and Increasing Slowly with any new routine, you can change your life in a way that sort of "sneaks up" on you and becomes permanent. Plan for the change to take place over six months, a year or even more. There will be times when you backslide or plateau, but that's pretty common; don't let it discourage you. It's better for your change to take a full two years and be successful, than for it to take two weeks and fail.

Exercise

New Routines

Think about the routines you want to introduce (p. 6). For each one, choose a small whole number, either in time or some other unit, that you can use as a starting point to introduce the routine into your life.

Then decide the amount you will add each time you want to increase. Finally, decide how often you will increase the amount. The first row uses the walking routine as an example.

Routine	Starting Whole Number Goal	Amount of Increase	Frequency of Increase	Final Goal
Walking	2 minutes 5x per week	1 minute	Each week	30 minutes 5x per week

Again, pick only *one* of these routines to introduce at one time. Beginning several at once is hardly starting small! When you reach your goal and maintain it for at least six months, start introducing the next routine into your life. It's okay if you plateau or even slip back to a smaller amount, but continue building up again when you are ready.

In the next chapter we will explore breaking large projects down into manageable pieces. (Did you mark down the next session on your calendar?)

Tool #3:
Break It Down into
Manageable Pieces

Many of us have a huge project or task that we avoid because the thought of doing it overwhelms us. The best way to deal with such a task is to break it down into a series of smaller tasks that aren't so menacing. By focusing on each piece, you can make progress without ending up feeling overwhelmed by the whole thing.

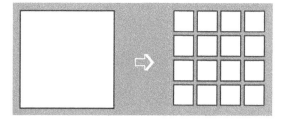

Good teachers do this for their students all the time when they assign research papers and large projects. They break the assignment up into smaller goals, and assign an interim due date for each step. You can do the same for your own large jobs.

The Typical Approach

One of the most common big tasks that many of us face is cleaning up our home or office space, and many people fail because they don't know how to tackle the project. For example, here's the way most people approach cleaning up a messy closet or cupboard: they open the door, select an item and decide whether to keep it or get rid of it. If they are going to keep it, they have to decide where it's going to go. If they are going to get rid of it, they have to decide whether to toss it, donate it or sell it.

They continue this process for a time, all the while creating piles on the floor. It seems that the closet isn't getting any emptier, but the room is getting messier, somehow managing to violate a basic rule of physics. Finally, they give up, jam everything back in to the closet and walk away in disgust, thinking maybe they'll come back to it another day when they have more time or energy. Sound familiar?

Divide and Conquer

I have a completely different approach to cleaning out a closet or any disorganized area. First, I get 8-10 of these nice Sterilite 66-Quart Latch Boxes. I particularly like these boxes because they are sturdy, stackable and transparent. Heavy cardboard boxes with lids are not quite as good, but they work okay and are free. For a task like this, I like the ones you can pick up at a liquor store because they are made to hold a lot of weight and they usually come with lids. You can, of course, get them from the store either empty or full!

Next I quickly empty the closet into the boxes. I make no decisions about what to do with each item; I just throw it in. The only exception is if the item is something I'm going to need in the next couple of weeks, in which case I set it aside. When a box fills up, I stack it on the previous one and then start filling up the next box. I continue doing this until the entire closet is emptied.

Now I've accomplished three things:

- I've broken the problem down into discrete units and I can go through the items one box at a time. Although the closet was overwhelming as a whole, each box is pretty manageable.
- By stacking the boxes, I've reduced the footprint of the mess to 1½ x 2 feet, which feels better.
- The closet is now a clean slate. Instead of trying to organize a messy space, I'm working with a clean space.

Now I can start from scratch, maybe put in some shelves, buy containers to hold things, and then start organizing the closet in a methodical way with only those items that belong there.

You can get control of your whole house this way. Clear out a section using the boxes, then go through the boxes one at a time before moving on to the next area.

But here's a warning if you use this method: Do NOT empty that closet into those boxes unless you have a plan for emptying them. Otherwise, in 102 years, I guarantee you those boxes will still be full of that stuff! So plan to set aside some time each day, maybe just 10 minutes, or some time each weekend to work your way through the boxes.

This is also a great way for kids to clean up a messy bedroom or playroom. Place everything that needs to be put away into the boxes, stacking them as they fill up. Then they are working in a clean room instead of one that is overwhelmingly messy. And again, the problem is broken down into manageable pieces. Depending upon the age of the child, you may need to help.

Tackling Other Big Jobs

If you are working on something bigger than a closet, like a garage, just tackle it one small section at a time. With a little thought, most large tasks can be broken down into smaller steps, but sometimes the easiest way to break down the task is with a timer. When I cleaned out my attic, I found it best just to work away at it for 20 minutes at a time, doing at least one 20-minute stint every weekend. That's also how I approached creating this book, by chipping away at it 20 minutes at a time.

Example: Grading Papers

When my friend Martha, a biology teacher at the local high school, has lab reports to grade, she divides them into stacks of 5 or 10 reports each. She concentrates on grading one stack at a time. As she completes each stack, she makes a mental note of the fraction of the total that she's completed, which gives her a sense of progress. She always finds the first reports take longer to grade than the rest of them, so when the first stack is done, Martha knows she's well on her way.

Summary

Break projects down into:

- Steps, like the steps of creating a report; or
- Discrete units, like using the boxes to clean out a space; or
- Chunks of time, using a timer.

Then concentrate only on the part you are working on. Don't think about the whole overwhelming project. They say the way to eat an elephant is one bite at a time. Well, that's how you tackle a huge job: one piece at a time.

Exercises

Tasks You Avoid

For each task listed on page 8, decide if it is something that you can break down. If so, do the following:

- **If you can break it down into units (like pages or square feet):** Decide on an appropriate unit and write it down.
- **If you can break it down into steps:** Write the first steps that must be completed. Be sure to pick steps that are a comfortable size. If a step feels too big, break it down into sub-steps.
- **Otherwise, break it down into time chunks.** If neither steps nor units is appropriate, almost any task can be broken down into chunks of time. Write the amount of time that you could comfortably work on the task you avoid.

Task	Break it down into one of the following:		
	Units	**Steps**	**Time**

Overwhelming Projects

Look at the overwhelming projects you listed on page 10. For each one, decide how you can break it down.

- **If you can break it down into units:** Decide on an appropriate unit and write it down.
- **If you can break it down into steps:** Write the first steps that must be completed. Be sure to pick steps that are a comfortable size. If a step feels too big, break it down into sub-steps.
- **Otherwise, break it down into time chunks.** If neither steps nor units is appropriate, almost any task can be broken down into chunks of time. Write the amount of time that you could comfortably work on the overwhelming project.

Project	Break it down into one of the following:		
	Units	**Steps**	**Time**

Next we'll look at figuring out when you are going to tackle these jobs (so the stuff isn't still in the boxes 102 years from now).

Don't forget to schedule when you are going to work on the next chapter.

Tool #4:
Make Your Decision Ahead of Time

We humans are not always good at making the right decision in the moment. If we're really hungry, we'll choose the double cheeseburger over the salad. If we're tired, we'll decide to watch TV instead of getting started on what we had wanted to accomplish. If we're having a good time, we'll tend to keep doing whatever it is we are doing even though we might need to get going on something else.

The Overeaters Anonymous Approach

Overeaters Anonymous knows dieters don't always make the best food choices in the moment. One component of their program is planning what to eat ahead of time. Each morning, a member calls his sponsor and together they decide exactly what he is going to eat that day. That way, there are no food decisions that happen in the moment. If someone brings doughnuts into the break room, the OA member has already decided that he is not going to have any. At lunch, he doesn't have to decide between the double cheeseburger and the broiled chicken because he already made that decision.

The next morning, the member checks in with the sponsor and lets her know how he did. That adds accountability to the plan, which adds to the probability of follow-through. Overeaters Anonymous knows there is a higher chance of success when people plan their eating instead of winging it.

Planning Ahead

When you make a plan to do something, decide on your goal ahead of time and be specific. Decide exactly:

- What you are going to do;
- How much you are going to do; and
- When you are going to do it.

Then write it down. If appropriate, write it on your calendar, just like you'd write down a doctor or dentist appointment, or like I've encouraged you to do for working on this program.

Example 1: Making Dinner on Time

Here's an example of how Making a Decision Ahead of Time can help create a new routine. In my house, I do the daily cooking and my husband does the dishes, and we like to eat around 6 p.m.

I'm not always great about judging how long things will take – just ask my husband about that – and if I'm working on something, like writing my newsletter or creating a new presentation, I don't like to stop. So in the past, as dinner time drew near, I'd tell myself that I still had plenty of time to get dinner on the table by 6. Around about 10 minutes to 6, I'd finally haul myself away from what I was doing to start dinner, and then I was shocked – shocked! – to find that dinner wasn't ready until nearly 7 p.m. My husband would just roll his eyes and say, "I can't believe you help people with time management for a living."

One day it occurred to me to use my own tool and Make My Decision Ahead of Time. If we want to eat at 6, I have to start dinner by 5! Seems obvious? Well, it wasn't to me in the moment! So now when 5 p.m. rolls around, I wrap up whatever I'm doing and start dinner. We're eating a lot closer to 6 p.m. most days. There are days that I slip back, but it's still significantly better than it used to be because now I've planned ahead as to when to quit working and start dinner.

Example 2: Finding a Job

When I first started working with Tricia, she'd been unemployed for almost 6 months and still didn't have her résumé together. The economy was sluggish and she knew that finding a job was going to be an uphill battle. So Tricia found herself wasting a fair amount of time on the computer looking at email, checking stock quotations and doing anything else she could think of to avoid the job search. Together, we started mapping out her days. First thing after breakfast, she would work on her résumé for 20 minutes, followed by 20 minutes (with the timer!) of looking at her email.

Midway through the morning, Tricia would do some networking, reaching out to 3 contacts (note the use of a whole number) either by phone or email, then she'd spend 20 more minutes on her résumé. We also planned out her afternoons, always with specific tasks at a specific time for a predetermined amount of time. After a week of this routine, Tricia had her résumé together and ready to send out.

We spent the remaining weeks of her job search making lists of people to call and companies to apply to, plus we included personal projects that were in need of attention. Tricia's list always included the day and time she was going to do each item. Her efforts paid off and she found a new job.

Example 3: Cleaning Out the House

Sarah wanted to get her house cleaned out so that she could put it on the market. She came home from work each day in the middle of the afternoon to put the dog out for a little while. We came up with a plan: while the dog was outside she would spend 30 minutes working on cleaning out using the bin technique I described in *Tool #3: Break It Down*. In less than a year, the house was cleaned out and on the market.

Example 4: Painting the Garage

Fred wanted to paint his garage, but kept putting it off. He was an older man, and didn't want to work outside when it was too hot or too cold. So we came up with a plan that on nice Saturday mornings, if the temperature was between 60-80 degrees, he would spend 2-3 hours working on it. He thought that might work, but then said, "I'm not sure how my wife will feel about my doing it a little at a time." I asked him, "How will your wife feel if you don't do it at all?" He agreed that my point was a valid one.

Summary

Would you go for a hike without having a plan or a map? Probably not – that's a good way to get lost. So don't wander through your life getting things done whenever you get to them. And don't make decisions at the last moment, or when you are tired, hungry or under pressure. Instead, plan ahead and make your decisions ahead of time. Decide exactly what you are going to do, how much you are going to do and when you are going to do it.

Exercises

New Routines

Plan ahead for each of your new routines (p. 6). Write down exactly what you are going to do, and when and how often you are going to do it. Then refer to the exercise on page 28 to decide how much you will do to start out. Remember, even though you are creating a plan for each new routine, only pick *one* to establish at a time.

Routine	What are you going to do?	When/How often will you do it?	Starting Out Amount

Tasks You Avoid

Fill out the table on the next page for each of the tasks you avoid (p. 8). The table you filled out on page 33 may be helpful.

Task	How often does it have to be done?	How long does it take to complete?	How many sessions do you want to do it in? (Do you want to break it down?)	How many steps/units/minutes per session?	When will you do it?
	___ Daily ___ Weekly ___ Monthly ___ Yearly ___ As needed ___ Other: ___				
	___ Daily ___ Weekly ___ Monthly ___ Yearly ___ As needed ___ Other: ___				
	___ Daily ___ Weekly ___ Monthly ___ Yearly ___ As needed ___ Other: ___				

Overwhelming Projects

On page 21, you created some whole number goals for each of your overwhelming projects and on page 34, you listed some ways to break them down into steps, units or time segments. Using these two concepts, come up with a plan to work on each one.

Project	When will you do the next three sessions?	How much (what steps, or how many units or minutes) will you do during each of these sessions?

Now that you've got your plan, it's time to commit to it, which we'll talk about in the next chapter. As always, be sure to schedule your next *Joy of Getting It Done* session.

Tool #5:
Make It a Commitment

When we decide to make a change in our lives, we often say something like "I'm gonna try to..." The word "try" gives us an out, and denotes a certain lack of seriousness we feel about making the change. What if we applied that same level of earnestness to marriage vows? The officiant would say to the groom, "Do you take this woman to be your lawfully wedded wife?" and the response would be, "I'll try" or even "Whatever" instead of "I DO!" And yes, although many marriages end in divorce, most couples do give a good effort to making it work first.

What is a commitment? Abraham Lincoln defined it perfectly when he said,

> *"Commitment is what transforms a promise into reality. It is the words that speak boldly of your intentions. And the actions which speak louder than the words.*
>
> *"It is making the time when there is none. Coming through time after time after time, year after year after year. Commitment is the stuff character is made of; the power to change the face of things. It is the daily triumph of integrity over skepticism."*

When you sign the mortgage papers for your home, you don't agree to make the payment if you have the money, or if it's convenient. You make a *commitment* to making a payment each month. Yet, when we decide to make a change, or make a New Year's resolution, the level of sincerity we often have is, "I'll try – if it isn't too hard." So how can we change our intentions into a real commitment?

Make a Public Declaration

Let people know what you are going to do and ask them to hold you accountable. Put yourself on the spot.

Your "public" declaration can be to a few people or a few hundred, but no matter what the number, tell people exactly what your plan is, specifically:

- What action you are going to take;
- When you are going to have it completed; and
- How they will know that you did it.

Example: Starting a Newsletter

When I started doing presentations, I collected the email addresses of people who wanted to be on my newsletter list. The problem was that I hadn't yet started doing newsletters. Time went on, and I was dragging my feet. I knew I needed to start writing, but I was afraid of the commitment of a monthly publication.

So at the beginning of October 2010, I sent an email out to all of the people on the list telling them to watch for my newsletter on the first of November. That gave me a month to put the first one together, so my plan was realistic, but I had put myself on the spot. I really had to follow through, especially given what I do for a living.

On the first of the next month, I sent out my first newsletter, and I've been sending them out regularly ever since.

Do It Despite Adversity

It's an amazing self-esteem boost when we find a way to forge ahead despite the fact that the going gets tough. It's easy to use adversity as an excuse for not following through. But when you find a way around the problem, that's the level of commitment that Lincoln was talking about. What if your life depended upon your following through? Even if it doesn't, act as though it does. When you are really determined to push through, you can be amazingly creative. If you planned to walk in the morning and it's raining, grab an umbrella or put on a raincoat and boots.

Have a Contingency Plan

But what if the conditions outside aren't safe, like during a hail or lightning storm? Obviously you don't want to endanger yourself. Let's face it, sometimes despite our very best intentions, life gets in the way.

If the conditions outside are too bad to take a walk, drive to the mall and walk there. Or put on an exercise video at home and follow along. The point is to find another way to do what you set out to do. Finding an equivalent alternative is another way of getting it done despite adversity.

Is It Ever Okay Just to Try without Actually <u>Committing</u>?

Absolutely! There are times that you aren't quite ready for a commitment, but you still want to dip your toe into the water. Maybe you don't want to make a full-fledged commitment because you aren't sure that you can realistically fulfill it. Sometimes making a commitment can be intimidating; it can even be a deterrent to change.

For example, the adult daughter of a dear friend of mine had to spend several months in a rehab facility that was far away from her family and friends, and she couldn't have access to email or the internet. Snail mail really cheered her up, so I decided that I would do my best to write her a letter each week. I wasn't ready to make it a commitment and tell anyone else because I wasn't sure I could follow through. Even so, I did manage to write to her 11 of the 12 weeks she was there.

On the other hand, if it hadn't been for making a commitment to doing my newsletter, I would still probably be waiting to start it.

My point here is that "Make It a Commitment" is a *tool*, not a *mandate*. In some cases, like starting my newsletter, it really helped me get going. In other cases, it might be a deterrent. As with every other tool in this book, it's up to you to decide which ones will help you to get the job done.

Are You Ready?

When you feel you are ready to commit to a change, make sure you have given it some serious thought over time. Like with any other commitment, don't make it impulsively or in an emotional moment of guilt or regret or even euphoria. As the old saying goes, "Marry in haste, repent at leisure."

Before you commit, ask yourself over the period of a few days or even weeks, "Am I really, really committed to making this happen?" You don't have to commit to a big change. As we saw with Tool #2, the change can be a very small one, just a beginning or a first step.

Summary

How serious are you about making a change? On a scale of 1 to 10, with 10 being completely committed to the change, what score would you give your commitment level? There's no right or wrong number, but being honest about how committed you are can help you decide if you are ready to make the change. If you are at a 9 or 10, making it a commitment can add to your probability of success.

Exercises

Incorporating a New Routine

Thinking about the one new routine that you want to start working on (p. 6), answer the following questions:

Name of New Routine:_____

1. Are you ready to make a commitment to start incorporating it into your life?

    ___ Yes (*skip to question #4*)   ___ No

2. Why don't you feel ready to commit to it at this time?

3. Do you think you will ever be ready to make a commitment for this routine?

___ Yes (When? _____)

___ No (*skip to "Committing to Tasks You Avoid"*)

4. When you are ready to commit to this routine, how will you announce it to people?

5. To whom will you announce it?

6. What are some of the things that could legitimately get in your way?

7. What's your contingency plan if something keeps you from doing your routine?

8. What are some of the excuses you could see yourself coming up with?

Committing to Tasks You Avoid

Thinking about each of the tasks you avoid (p. 8), answer the following questions:

Task #1: _____

1. Would making a commitment to this task help you to face it?

   ___ Yes (*skip to question #4*)   ___ No

2. Why not?

3. Do you think you will ever be ready to make a commitment for this task?

   ___ Yes (When? _____)

   ___ No (*skip to Task #2*)

4. How will you announce making a commitment to this task?

5. To whom will you announce it?

6. What are some of the things that could legitimately get in your way?

7. What's your contingency plan if something keeps you from working on the task when you say you will?

8. What are some of the excuses you could see yourself coming up with?

Task #2: _____

1. Would making a commitment to this task help you to face it?

    ___ Yes (*skip to question #4*)   ___ No

2. Why not?

3. Do you think you will ever be ready to make a commitment for this task?

   ____ Yes (When? _____)

   ____ No (*skip to Task #3*)

4. How will you announce making a commitment to this task?

5. To whom will you announce it?

6. What are some of the things that could legitimately get in your way?

7. What's your contingency plan if something keeps you from working on the task when you say you will?

8. What are some of the excuses you could see yourself coming up with?

Task #3: _____

1. Would making a commitment to this task help you to face it?

    ___ Yes (*skip to question #4*)   ___ No

2. Why not?

3. Do you think you will ever be ready to make a commitment for this task?

    ___ Yes (When? _____)

    ___ No (s*kip to "Committing to Overwhelming Projects"*)

4. How will you announce making a commitment to this task?

5. To whom will you announce it?

6. What are some of the things that could legitimately get in your way?

7. What's your contingency plan if something keeps you from working on the task when you say you will?

8. What are some of the excuses you could see yourself coming up with?

Committing to Overwhelming Projects

Thinking about each of your projects (p. 10), answer the following questions:

Project #1: _____

1. Are you ready to make a commitment to completing the project?

    ____ Yes (*skip to question #4*)   ____ No

2. Why don't you feel ready to commit to it at this time?

3. Do you think you will ever be ready to make a commitment to this project?

    ____ Yes (When? _____)

    ____ No (*skip to Project #2*)

4. When you are ready to commit to this project, how will you announce it to people?

5. To whom will you announce it?

6. What are some of the things that could legitimately get in your way?

7. What's your contingency plan if something keeps you from working on the project?

8. What are some of the excuses you could see yourself coming up with?

Project #2: _____

1. Are you ready to make a commitment to completing the project?

    ____ Yes *(skip to question #4)*   ____ No

2. Why don't you feel ready to commit to it at this time?

3. Do you think you will ever be ready to make a commitment to this project?

    ____ Yes (When?) _____)

    ____ No *(skip to Project #3)*

4. When you are ready to commit to this project, how will you announce it to people?

5. To whom will you announce it?

6. What are some of the things that could legitimately get in your way?

7. What's your contingency plan if something keeps you from working on the project?

8. What are some of the excuses you could see yourself coming up with?

Project #3: _____

1. Are you ready to make a commitment to completing the project?

    ___ Yes (*skip to question #4*)   ___ No

2. Why don't you feel ready to commit to it at this time?

3. Do you think you will ever be ready to make a commitment to this project?

    ___ Yes (When? _____)

    ___ No (*skip to the end of the exercises*)

4. When you are ready to commit to this project, how will you announce it to people?

5. To whom will you announce it?

6. What are some of the things that could legitimately get in your way?

7. What's your contingency plan if something keeps you from working on the project?

8. What are some of the excuses you could see yourself coming up with?

In the next chapter, we'll look at ways to create a new routine by adding it to an existing routine.

Remember to schedule when you will work on it.

Tool #6:
Make It Part of an Existing Routine

Some people react negatively to the idea of creating routines. I once had an audience member at a presentation I was giving tell me she was afraid that establishing routines would ruin her spontaneity. But the truth is that routines free us up. When we have a routine, we don't have to think about it, and our minds are free to think about more important things.

For example, if you didn't have a routine, you'd have to make the same decisions every morning: Do I take my shower first or brush my teeth? Do I get dressed before or after breakfast? Decisions can be exhausting, and making the same ones over and over again is a waste of time and energy.

When you are establishing a new routine, make it part of a routine that is already in place. You can do the new behavior before or after the established routine; the important thing is to do them one right after the other and always in the same order.

Doing It at the Same Time Every Day

Think of one of the routines that you'd like to start doing regularly. Then, think of something that you already do regularly at the same time each day. Finally, attach the new activity to the currently-existing one, by always doing the new activity either immediately before or after the existing one.

Example: Paperwork

Many of my clients want to get a handle on their paperwork, both getting through the pile on their desk and keeping on top of the new paper coming in daily.

Hopefully you eat breakfast every day, so that's an already-established routine. So a new routine would be spending some time on paperwork every day immediately after you get up from the breakfast table.

And remember Tool #2 – *Start Small and Increase Slowly*. So if your goal is 20 minutes of paperwork each day, start out doing just a few minutes and work up slowly.

The important thing is that every single time you finish breakfast, you go straight to your desk and work on paperwork. Even if you only do it for a few minutes, it's building a habit.

Once the routine is established, you can extend your time slowly, maybe by just 2 minutes a week until you've built up to 20-30 minutes each day. If there is a morning that you can't do the full amount, try to do at least a few minutes to keep the routine going.

This is a routine I've established for myself, and it really does keep me on top of the paper chase. However, there's no one-size-fits-all here. You have to decide upon routines that work for you.

Doing It before or after a Specific Activity

Routines don't have to be tied to something that you do at the same time every day. They can be tied to a specific action, something that you do regularly, but at different times throughout the day or week.

Example: Hanging Up My Coat

When I was a kid, we had an entrance hall with an armchair and a closet.

Whenever I came in the house with my coat on, my routine was to throw the coat on the chair, much to my mom's dismay. So she established the routine of calling me out to the hall to hang up the coat anytime she found it on the chair. It was a routine all right, but not a very good one because she resented always having to nag me to hang the coat up, and I resented being interrupted to do it. Like most kids, I just didn't get the concept that it would have been easier to hang it up in the first place.

One day my mom got smart and decided it was time for a new and better routine (and no, she didn't remove the chair from the hall). For a couple of weeks, every time she heard the front door close when I entered the house, she hurried out to the hall to stop me from throwing the coat on the chair. So for me, there was a new routine established – when I took off the coat, I immediately hung it in the closet.

After a week or two, the new routine had taken root. I never again threw the coat on the chair. Hanging it up had just become second nature. Even when I became an adult and moved away, when I visited my parents' home, I always hung up my coat in that closet. I didn't even think about doing it. That's how entrenched a routine can become.

"Binding" the New Routine to an Established Routine

Another way of linking one routine to another one is to *bind* the two routines together, which means that you always do both of them at the same time. This is not the same as multitasking. Binding two activities only works if one of the activities is fairly mindless, like cleaning up clutter, and the other activity doesn't engage your hands, such as listening to a favorite television show.

Example 1: The Fix-It Basket

It's not uncommon for people to have a basket of things that need mending, maybe a blouse that needs a button or a broken item that needs to be glued. In general, these things never get fixed, worn or used again and eventually get tossed.

I have a basket like that, but my stuff actually does get fixed. I do it by binding one of my favorite weekly TV programs to fixing the stuff in the basket. I *do not allow* myself to watch that show unless I'm working on these items. It's a great way to do boring activities while I keep my mind occupied, and I love the feeling of accomplishment I have when the program is over. Now that the routine is established, I find I really enjoy doing it. In fact I look forward to it.

Example 2: Clutter and Laundry

There are lots of ways to bind two activities together. I have a head-set for my phone and, when I get a call from a friend, I put on the headset and use that chatting time to do mundane tasks like picking up the clutter around the house or folding the laundry. Sometimes I get so engrossed in the conversation that I don't even notice what I'm doing. I've honestly had times that I've finished the call and then gone up to the bedroom to put away laundry, only to find out that I had already done it while I was  talking! Most cordless phones have headset jacks now, and you can pick up a headset for under $25 at most stores that sell electronics.

A friend of mine said, "I tried talking on the phone while I worked on things, but it didn't work."

"What did you do while you were talking?" I asked.

"I was trying to pay my bills," she replied. Hmmm.

Summary

Attaching a new routine to an existing routine can be a very effective way to get that new routine going. Find some time directly before, during or after an already-established activity, and slip your new routine in there. And don't forget Tool #2 – *Start Small and Increase Slowly.*

Exercises

New Routines

For **one** of the new routines (p. 6) that you want to incorporate into your life, decide if you can tie it to an existing routine. You may want to refer back to the exercise you completed on page 38.

Down the road, when the first new routine is firmly established, you can come back and fill out the next row, deciding on how you will incorporate the next routine.

New Routine	Existing Routine	How often do you do the existing routine?	How will you add the new routine to the existing routine?
		___ Daily ___ Weekly ___ Monthly ___ Yearly ___ As needed ___ Other: _____	___ Do it right before ___ Do it right after ___ Do it during (bind them)
		___ Daily ___ Weekly ___ Monthly ___ Yearly ___ As needed ___ Other: _____	___ Do it right before ___ Do it right after ___ Do it during (bind them)
		___ Daily ___ Weekly ___ Monthly ___ Yearly ___ As needed ___ Other: _____	___ Do it right before ___ Do it right after ___ Do it during (bind them)

Tasks You Avoid

For each of the tasks you avoid that you identified on page 8, decide if you can tie it to an existing routine. You may want to refer back to the exercise you completed on page 39.

Task Name	Existing Routine	How often do you do the existing routine?	How will you add the task to the existing routine?
		___ Daily ___ Weekly ___ Monthly ___ Yearly ___ As needed ___ Other _____	___ Do it right before ___ Do it right after ___ Do it during (bind them)
		___ Daily ___ Weekly ___ Monthly ___ Yearly ___ As needed ___ Other _____	___ Do it right before ___ Do it right after ___ Do it during (bind them)
		___ Daily ___ Weekly ___ Monthly ___ Yearly ___ As needed ___ Other _____	___ Do it right before ___ Do it right after ___ Do it during (bind them)

Any plan can go awry when distractions get in the way. In the next chapter we'll talk about how to keep that from happening.

(Did you mark your calendar?)

Tool #7:
Deal with Distractions

When you're working on something, distractions can slow you down or derail you altogether. And if what you are doing is something that you don't particularly enjoy, those distractions can really be enticing. To deal with them effectively, it helps if you anticipate what they'll be ahead of time, then modify your environment to reduce them to a minimum.

Implementing the following ideas before you start a task can reduce the amount of distractions you will have to fend off. Ben Franklin was right: "An ounce of prevention is worth a pound of cure." Here are some strategies that can help to prevent distractions from happening while you are working.

Close Your Door

If you don't have a door, display some sort of "Don't interrupt me" sign or signal. I know someone who puts crime scene tape across the opening of his cubicle when he doesn't want to be interrupted.

Close Your Email

If you don't close it, at least turn off the "New Email" notification signal. Email is a really tempting distraction, especially if what you're doing is difficult or you're not enjoying it. In fact it's good to check email only at pre-planned intervals throughout the day.

Log Out of Social Media Programs

Log out of Facebook, Twitter or any other social media programs that might tempt you.

Teach Children to Wait

If you are working at home around your children, they can be taught to wait their age in minutes. When your 4-year-old wants your attention, set a timer for 4 minutes and tell him that he will have to wait until the timer goes off. Be fair; when the 4 minutes is up, attend to his need. Doing this teaches your child both patience and respect for others' time.

Ignore Your Phone

Don't answer the phone, or even better, turn the ringer off. If you can't do this, decide ahead of time whose calls you will answer. You probably want to pick it up if it's your child's school, the doctor or your boss. But beware of friends and relatives who call to chat – save that for later.

Similarly, silence your cell phone, especially the texting notification. Texting is a huge distraction in our lives. We're becoming infinitely available, and infinitely interruptible. We can't work efficiently if we're constantly stopping to read and send texts.

Plan Ahead

Get your coffee or tea before you start, and gather everything you need to work on the task at hand. Having to stop to get things can really slow you down.

Get Comfortable

Make sure you are as comfortable as possible before you start. Being uncomfortable can be a significant distraction.

Set a Timer

Finally, set a timer for a specific period of time and do not succumb to the temptation of interruptions before it goes off. It's amazing how much easier it is to avoid getting distracted when you focus yourself for a specific period of time with a timer. You know that when it goes off, you can deal with the other things; you aren't putting them off indefinitely. Alternatively, instead of using a timer, you can pick a whole number goal.

Reaching Your Goal

After you've managed to get a good chunk of work in, interruption-free, is there anything wrong with taking a break with a few minutes on social media or a chat on the phone? Not as long as it's time-limited.

If you know that you can disappear into email, the internet or YouTube videos, set the timer to limit the amount of time you spend on your break.

Distracting People

Finally, what about those "Got a minute?" people – you know, those people who come into your office or cubicle when you are in the middle of something and don't take the hint when you tell them you are busy?

I'm not talking about the people who come in, ask you a quick question and leave. I'm talking about the ones who want to sit and chat and waste their time and yours.

When one of those people comes into your office or cubicle, the first thing to do is to stand up. This sends the message that you are not going to settle in for a nice long chat. Most people will get the hint, but if they don't get it soon, walk out of your office with them – the important thing is to get them out of your space.

Once they're out, find a way to interrupt them (I know that can be hard). Tell them you're sorry and you'd love to continue talking, but you really have to get back to work. Then quickly walk back to your desk. Few people will be so pushy as to follow you.

The important thing is to have a plan to deal with the "Got a minute?" people. Otherwise it can be very hard to extricate yourself.

Summary

The secret to dealing with distractions is to anticipate them and plan ahead for them. Before you start working, think of the ways that interruptions might happen. Then set up your environment to minimize the chances that they will occur. Also, think about how to deal with distractions if they happen despite your best efforts to avoid them.

Exercises

On the next three pages, write down up to three anticipated distractions for each of your goals. Then write down how you could decrease the chances of each one happening. Finally, write down how you could deal with the distraction to minimize its impact if it occurs.

New Routines

New Routine (list on page 6)	Possible Distraction	How to Prevent or Decrease Odds of Its Occurring	How to Deal with It If It Does Occur

Tasks You Avoid

Task (list on page 8)	Possible Distraction	How to Prevent or Decrease Odds of Its Occurring	How to Deal with It If It Does Occur

Overwhelming Projects

Project (list on page 10)	Possible Distraction	How to Prevent or Decrease Odds of Its Occurring	How to Deal with It If It Does Occur

Sometimes having a carrot in front of you can help to motivate you to stay on task. In the next chapter we'll explore some ways to reward yourself for working towards your goals.

Be sure to schedule your next session on your calendar.

Tool #8:
Reward Yourself

How can you motivate yourself to do something that just doesn't appeal to you, but that you know is important to do or complete? Consider giving yourself a reward when you finish it. Reward systems can take many forms and can be surprisingly simple to implement.

Premack's Principle

In the 1960s, David Premack, Ph.D., a psychologist at the University of Pennsylvania, created Premack's Principle, which states that "more probable behaviors will reinforce less probable behaviors."[1] A "more probable behavior" is something that you do naturally because you have to or because you enjoy it. A "less probable behavior" is something you are trying to incorporate into your life, that maybe you don't enjoy or that doesn't come naturally to you. You use the more probable behavior as a carrot for the less probable one. Your mom used Premack's Principle when she said you couldn't have dessert (the more probable behavior) if you didn't eat your vegetables (the less probable behavior).

Although very simple, Premack's Principle can be a powerful tool for change. Think of the more probable behavior as your reward. You pair a behavior, or an activity, that you know you'll do with something that you want to accomplish. The more probable activity can be something that you know you will reliably do (like leaving for work) or something you really enjoy (like reading a book).

Example 1: Dealing with Paperwork

In my own life, I use Premack's Principle to keep the pile of paper on my desk at bay. I know that I will always read my email. That's the high probability activity. So I don't allow myself to read email until either I've spent 20 minutes in the morning working on the paper pile or I get through the pile, whichever comes first.

Example 2: Getting Dressed

Valerie found that once she went downstairs in the morning in her bathrobe, she tended to stay in her pajamas most of the day, which she didn't like doing. So we identified going downstairs as the high probability activity and getting dressed as the low probability activity. We came up with a plan where she could stay upstairs in the morning as long as she wanted, but she wouldn't go downstairs until she was dressed. Using Premack's Principle can be that simple.

Example 3: Doing the Laundry

Emily had a full-time job. She let the laundry go until the weekend, then was stuck at home every Saturday or Sunday getting it done. "If only I could do it on weeknights," she lamented, "but somehow I just can't seem to get it started." She told me that starting a load was the only problem. Once it was in the washer, she had no trouble transferring it to the dryer, then folding it and putting it away.

We came up with a plan: if there was a load of laundry that needed to go in, she couldn't eat her dinner (the high probability activity) until the laundry was in the washer (the low probability activity). It wasn't as if she had to go to the river and beat the clothes on a rock while she was nearly fainting from hunger; she told me it took her less than five minutes to get the clothes started. When I talked to her the next week, she reported that her laundry was all done by Friday night and she had her weekend free.

Bribe Yourself

Use Premack's Principle to bribe yourself – that is, to pick something you enjoy doing as a reward for doing the behavior that does not come naturally to you. It doesn't have to be something big or special, just something that you like and do regularly, like reading a book or going on social media. And you don't have to do the rewarding activity directly after the target activity you are trying to cultivate. For example, you could say, "I only get to watch TV tonight if I clean off my desk before I leave work for the day."

Example: Studying

When Beth, a college student, has an assignment that she's really struggling to stay focused on, she bribes herself with the help of her timer. She does 20-30 minutes of focused work, followed by 10-15 minutes of a computer activity she enjoys. 20-30 minutes feels manageable for a task she really doesn't like, and there's always a respite that's never far away.

A Word of Caution

Premack's Principle is powerful but also fragile, especially at first. Once you slip and allow yourself the more probable activity without doing the less probable one, the principle's effectiveness is pretty well compromised. So think carefully and realistically about the change and reward you are going to pair up.

Remember to start small with the change you are introducing. Aim for consistency with holding out the reward for the behavior change, and slowly increase the amount of the change over time. Down the road, when your change is well-established, an occasional "cheat" won't derail you, but hang tough in the beginning. Make the pairing a commitment!

Big Ticket Rewards

You can also reward yourself with something special that you wouldn't otherwise get around to treating yourself to. Maybe you're looking for an excuse to go out on the town. Find a project, and use the night out as a carrot to entice yourself to complete the project.

You can also reward yourself with something big. Is there something really special that you want? Maybe something that you've been wanting to buy or a special trip you'd like to take? Obviously you can't say, "Okay, I walked 15 minutes this morning, so now I get to go to Bermuda." Instead, earn your reward by using the equivalent of a sticker chart. We generally think of these as being only for children, but the truth is they can be very effective motivators for adults.

Draw a grid on a piece of paper with a specific number of squares on it, maybe 25 or 50 or 100. The bigger the reward, the more squares you'll want to do, but you probably want to limit it to 100 or so. Each time you complete a small goal, put a check mark in one of the squares. It's a great visual way to chart your progress, and when the squares are filled, you've earned your reward. You can use this to help establish a new habit, like "Each time I walk for 10 minutes or more, I'll check off a box." Or to work your way through a project, like "Each time I clean out one drawer in the kitchen, I earn a square" or "Each time I spend 20 minutes cleaning out the attic, I can check off a square." There are many ways to do it.

Roberto earns a certain number of checks per task, not according to how hard the task actually is, but how hard it feels to him. When he earns 100 checks, he treats himself to a special day trip.

Be sure to give yourself the reward when you've earned it. It's amazing how often people work hard for a reward, then don't give it to themselves or up the ante!

Chore	Check Marks Earned			
Put away the laundry	✔			
Vacuum 1 room	✔	✔		
Clean the bathroom	✔	✔	✔	
10 minutes on clutter	✔	✔		
10 minutes on paper pile	✔	✔		
Plan a meal	✔	✔		
Go food shopping	✔	✔	✔	✔
Donate bag of clothes	✔	✔	✔	
Recycle 1 bag of paper	✔	✔		
Mend 1 item of clothing	✔	✔		

Additional Motivation

For particularly difficult tasks or habits, you can double up the rewards. For example, don't allow yourself to watch TV in the evening unless you've worked out during the day, and when you've worked out 30 times, you get to do something special.

Summary

If you set them up correctly and follow through, rewards – from simple everyday activities to special events – can be powerful motivators for change. They don't have to be complicated or elaborate. You can apply Premack's Principle to use everyday behaviors or use things you regularly enjoy doing as motivators. Or you can use a chart to earn a big ticket reward.

Exercises

Write down three high probability activities that you reliably do on a regular basis, like eating dinner or going downstairs in the morning. Then write down a low probability activity that you can pair with each one of them. The low probability activities can be from your list of new routines (p. 6), tasks you avoid (p. 8) or overwhelming projects (p. 10). The pairings you create should have the same regularity. That is, pair things you want to do daily with high probability activities you do daily, pair things you want to do weekly with high probability activities you want to do weekly and so on.

High Probability Activity (Something you do reliably on a regular basis)	Low Probability Activity (New routine, task you avoid or overwhelming project)

Write down a few simple activities that you enjoy on a regular basis. Then write down the tasks or activities that you can use to earn these rewards. Again, pair things that have the same regularity.

High Probability Activity (Something you enjoy doing)	Low Probability Activity (New routine, task you avoid or overwhelming project)

Write down some "big ticket" rewards, some goals that you want to accomplish and how you will use a chart to earn that special reward.

"Big Ticket" Reward	Goal (New routine, task you avoid or overwhelming project)	Number of squares in chart	How much will you do to check off one box?

Now go back through these exercises, look at the different ideas that you came up with and decide which ones you will implement. Write your plan down in the chart on the next page. Remember to only implement one of your new routines at a time.

Goal (New routine, task you avoid or overwhelming project)	Reward (Something you do reliably or enjoy doing or "big ticket")	Notes on how you will implement this plan.

In the next chapter, we examine "black holes" — those activities that suck us in and waste our time.

If you are going to stop for today, remember to mark your calendar for the next session.

Tool #9:
Avoid Your Personal Black Holes

A black hole is a region in space that has so much mass that nothing, not even light, can escape. Black holes are great metaphors for those activities that suck us in so strongly that once we start doing them, we just can't seem to escape.

What Sucks You In?

For some people, it's the computer, especially social media, games and YouTube. Some people find television to be a black hole. Once they sit down in front of the TV, the useful part of the day is over. When we indulge in one of our black holes, it's almost as if we gain 1,000 pounds and we just don't have the physical strength to move away from it.

Are You Enjoying or Avoiding?

While we may like most of the activities that are our black holes, there are some that we engage in not because we enjoy them, but because we are avoiding doing something we don't want to do.

Example 1: Coffee and the Morning Paper

Allen had very flexible hours at his job. When he had a meeting or appointment in the morning, he was always on time. But if nothing was scheduled, he would sit down with the newspaper and a cup of coffee. He'd read everything of interest while he drank his coffee. Then he'd get a second cup, which he didn't really want, and waste time reading things he had no interest in. As a result, he would get to the office much later than he liked.

He estimated that it took him about 45 minutes to read the things he cared about, so we agreed he would set the timer to limit the reading to that time period. In many cases, setting the timer to limit an activity is sufficient, and he thought that would work. However, the next week, when I asked him how it went, he reported that the plan had failed. At that point we realized that the newspaper was a black hole for him; it was controlling his morning. I asked Allen if he could put off reading the paper until the evening, and he was okay with that.

It's not always obvious when something is a black hole. If you have an activity that you can limit with a timer, then it's probably not one. The question is, are you controlling the activity, or is it controlling you? Black holes for most people are like alcoholics with a drink. There's just no stopping once they get started.

Does this mean that you should never engage in an activity you enjoy because it's a black hole? Of course not. Just be sure to plan to do it at an appropriate time. You can even use your black hole as a reward for having accomplished a goal. However, beware – indulging in a black hole at the end of the day can result in missed sleep as you stay up all hours of the night enjoying it. Better to schedule it as a leisure activity to enjoy on a day off.

Example 2: Online Games

Emily would take her iPad to bed with her intending to read a downloaded book, then end up staying up very late playing *Words With Friends* and missing sleep. To solve the problem, she stopped taking the iPad upstairs with her at night. Instead, she went back to reading good old-fashioned books in bed, and that solved the problem. Sometimes physical separation is the best approach to avoiding something that we have trouble controlling.

Summary

Now that you know about black holes, be aware of them. Sometimes you need to relax with something mindless. But if you find that you are often wasting time with a particular activity, or you feel that it's controlling you, it's a probably a black hole just sucking you in. You might need to plan a specific time to enjoy it or in some cases, you might need to do all you can to stay away from it altogether.

Exercise

Think about what your personal black holes are, and list two of them in the chart on the next page. Then fill out the rest of the chart for each one. Note that your black holes may be the same as the activities you identified on page 22 (*Losing Yourself*).

Making real change, including avoiding your personal black holes, can be tough to do on your own. In the next chapter, we'll talk about getting the support you need to succeed.

Have you scheduled a time to work on it?

Black Hole	How much do you enjoy this activity?	How much does it interfere with achieving your goals?	How much does it control *you*?	Do you do this because you enjoy it, or for avoidance?	Is this something you can do, or should you avoid it completely?
	___ A lot ___ Fair amount ___ Somewhat ___ A little ___ Very little ___ Not at all	___ A lot ___ Fair amount ___ Somewhat ___ A little ___ Very little ___ Not at all	___ A lot ___ Fair amount ___ Somewhat ___ A little ___ Very little ___ Not at all	___ Always do be-cause I enjoy it ___ Usually do be-cause I enjoy it ___ 50/50 ___ Usually do for avoidance ___ Always do for avoidance	___ I can do this occasionally. ___ I can do this occasionally, but only if I plan how much I'll do ahead of time. ___ I should avoid this completely.
	___ A lot ___ Fair amount ___ Somewhat ___ A little ___ Very little ___ Not at all	___ A lot ___ Fair amount ___ Somewhat ___ A little ___ Very little ___ Not at all	___ A lot ___ Fair amount ___ Somewhat ___ A little ___ Very little ___ Not at all	___ Always do be-cause I enjoy it ___ Usually do be-cause I enjoy it ___ 50/50 ___ Usually do for avoidance ___ Always do for avoidance	___ I can do this occasionally. ___ I can do this occasionally, but only if I plan how much I'll do ahead of time. ___ I should avoid this completely.

Tool #10:
Get Support

Change is hard, no doubt about it. Some people can make and maintain a significant change on their own, but for many of us, it takes the support of others to keep us on the straight and narrow, especially when the going gets tough. I often hear people tell me that they "should" be able to achieve their goals on their own. But there's a reason that support groups are so popular: it's because so many people have a higher rate of successful change when they have oth-

ers who will support them, encourage them and hold them accountable. It makes a lot more sense to attain your goals with support than spend your life not achieving them on your own!

Get Support by Announcing Your Intentions

There is some research that suggests telling people your goals makes you less likely to attain them. One study[1] found that people who tell others their intentions actually follow through less often than those who don't tell others. According to this study, telling your co-workers about your New Year's resolution leads to what the author calls a "premature sense of completeness." In other words, you feel so good telling everyone your intentions that you don't need to actually carry them out to get the emotional reward. So telling people can sometimes backfire.

But there's a big difference between getting that "feel-good" by telling everyone, "My New Year's resolution is to get in shape," and saying to a specific person or people, "First thing Monday morning, I'm going to the gym to lift weights for 15 minutes. And then, I'm going to email you and let you know that I did it."

When you tell your support person or people what your intentions are, make them very specific.

Tell them:

- What action you are going to take;
- How much you are going to do;
- When you are going to do it; and
- How they will know that you did it.

Let them know you want them to hold you accountable. Tell them that if you do not follow through, they need to ask you why, and if your reason sounds like an excuse, they need to call you on it.

Find a Buddy

Another way of getting support is to work on your goal with another person. For example, plan to meet at a specific time each day for a walk. Take turns helping each other clean out a cluttered area in each of your homes. Get together with a friend to plan a week's worth of healthy meals, then go shopping for the ingredients together. Before you part, be sure to schedule the next session.

Support Groups

Structured support groups can be very, well, supportive. You might want to join an established group, such as a weight loss group, a fitness team or class at your local gym or Y, or one of the support groups provided at houses of worship.

Alternatively, you can start your own group. Find one or more friends who have a common goal and who work well together to help each other. Or create a group on *www.meetup.com*. Meet regularly, either in person or via a conference call. There are many excellent free conference call services out there. You can find them on the internet.

LaLeche League International, the breastfeeding support organization, started with a group of seven mothers who wanted to support each other in nursing their babies back in the 1950s when most babies were bottle-fed. But your group doesn't have to be the beginning of a worldwide organization to be successful!

Example: A Workplace Productivity Support Group

I was fortunate enough to work at AT&T Bell Laboratories back when it was one of the research meccas of the world. My colleagues were among the best and brightest in their fields and passionate about their work. Yet even these accomplished professionals found themselves struggling with time management and procrastination. A group of us decided to start meeting regularly to set goals. By mutual agreement, we were a tough crowd. Goals were considered *commitments*. If you didn't follow through on your commitment, you had to tell the group what you could have done differently so as to complete your goal. Our group's productivity immediately increased, as did job satisfaction. People were much happier when they knew they were being held accountable.

A major perk of working in our division was infinite flextime. No one cared what hours you worked as long as the job got done. This was a blessing for some but a curse for others. One member of our group, Cindy, cruised into work around 5 p.m. each evening and worked late into the night. Management didn't care; she did excellent work and always got things done on time. But Cindy wasn't happy about her chosen work hours. The problem was that she would get distracted at home, spending time on whatever came into her field of vision. Without having to be at work at a certain time, she wasted her day at home doing trivial things she didn't really care about. So Cindy made a commitment to our group that she was going to be at work at 9:00 a.m. sharp every day. She wasn't going to get there at 9:05 or even 9:01; she would be in her chair by 9:00 a.m. on the dot – as I said, we were serious! I'll never forget the day I looked out my window to see her bolting across the parking lot to make it on time. She did, and was very pleased with her new schedule.

We used our group to set personal goals as well, and Cindy made several commitments to us just before we took off for the Christmas holidays. I received an excited phone call from her during that time. "I can't believe it!" she said. "I can't believe how much energy I have because of this group! It's wonderful. I'm so happy!" Being part of our tough little group really changed Cindy's life.

Who Are Your Support People?

Support can be one person or a group. They need to be people you can turn to, who will help you through the rough parts and keep you honest if you start to backslide. You don't want to choose people who are harsh and critical, but you certainly don't want what I call "poor baby" people either – those folks who will accept your excuses and thereby unintentionally support your failure. Our support group at Bell Labs worked so well because we agreed that we were serious about accountability.

You'll need support people who will "hold your feet to the fire" when it would be easier for you to cave in; people who will encourage you, gently nudge you and see through your excuses.

You can hire support people. Using professional support providers can be highly effective because they are trained to provide support, ideas, knowledge and accountability. Nutritionists, athletic trainers, professional organizers, psychotherapists, life coaches and ADHD coaches are all examples of people who are trained to help you in your quest for change. They can function as cheerleaders, educators and mirrors – reflecting back to you what they observe, helping you to learn about yourself and discover the roots of what is holding you back.

Hiring a Coach

Life coaches and ADHD coaches are trained specifically to help people find the obstacles blocking a desired change. They help people examine beliefs, mindsets and habits that might be getting in the way. They have no agenda, so can often be more objective than a friend or family member can be. Most people find working with a coach to be very effective for achieving goals.

Before you hire a life coach or an ADHD coach, make sure you know what you want to achieve with coaching. Interview several coaches that have been certified by the International Coach Federation (ICF) or the Center for Credentialing & Education (CCE). Certification indicates that the coach has been trained and has demonstrated a specific level of proficiency defined by the credentialing organization. The ICF website, *www.coachfederation.org*, and the CCE website, *www.cce-global.org*, both have listings of certified coaches. The ICF website also has suggestions for questions to ask a potential coach.

You don't have to be constrained by geography. Most life coaches meet with their clients by phone, but some do meet in person. As a coach, I work with all of my clients by phone. I find people who are already struggling with managing their time don't need the overhead of having one more place to be. But that doesn't work for everyone. If you feel you need to work with someone in person, you can search either site for coaches in your local area.

After you've interviewed a few potential coaches, choose the one that feels like the best fit.

Summary

No matter where you find support, be it a group, a friend or a professional, don't be afraid to reach out when you are looking to change your life. It can make the difference between success and failure.

Exercises

Look at each of your goals and decide if support would help you achieve it. If so, decide who that support will be and how it will be set up. Fill out the following chart for each one.

New Routines

(Choose one from your list on page 6.)

Routine	Would support be helpful?	What form would the support take?	Who are the people who would form your support group?
	___ Yes ___ No (skip to the next goal)	___ Specific group of friends or associates to tell your intentions ___ One or two buddies to work together on the same goal ___ Join an established support group ___ Create your own support group (to meet regularly) ___ Hire a professional ___ Other: _____ _____	

Tasks You Avoid

Task (list on page 8)	Would support be helpful?	What form would the support take?	Who are the people who would form your support group?
	___ Yes ___ No (skip to the next goal)	___ Specific group of friends or associates to tell your intentions ___ One or two buddies to work together on the same goal ___ Join an established support group ___ Create your own support group (to meet regularly) ___ Hire a professional ___ Other: _____ _____	
	___ Yes ___ No (skip to the next goal)	___ Specific group of friends or associates to tell your intentions ___ One or two buddies to work together on the same goal ___ Join an established support group ___ Create your own support group (to meet regularly) ___ Hire a professional ___ Other: _____ _____	

Task	Would support be helpful?	What form would the support take?	Who are the people who would form your support group?
	___ Yes ___ No (skip to the next goal)	___ Specific group of friends or associates to tell your intentions ___ One or two buddies to work together on the same goal ___ Join an established support group ___ Create your own support group (to meet regularly) ___ Hire a professional ___ Other: _____ _____	

Overwhelming Projects

Project (list on page 10)	Would support be helpful?	What form would the support take?	Who are the people who would form your support group?
	___ Yes ___ No (skip to the next goal)	___ Specific group of friends or associates to tell your intentions ___ One or two buddies to work together on the same goal ___ Join an established support group ___ Create your own support group (to meet regularly) ___ Hire a professional ___ Other: _____ _____	
	___ Yes ___ No (skip to the next goal)	___ Specific group of friends or associates to tell your intentions ___ One or two buddies to work together on the same goal ___ Join an established support group ___ Create your own support group (to meet regularly) ___ Hire a professional ___ Other: _____ _____	

Project	Would support be helpful?	What form would the support take?	Who are the people who would form your support group?
	___ Yes ___ No (skip to the end of the exercises)	___ Specific group of friends or associates to tell your intentions ___ One or two buddies to work together on the same goal ___ Join an established support group ___ Create your own support group (to meet regularly) ___ Hire a professional ___ Other: _____ _____	

You've now gone through the 10 *Joy of Getting It Done* tools, and hopefully given some thought to how each one of them can help you achieve your goals. We'll pull it all together in the next chapter, so be sure to mark your calendar now for this final session.

Part 3
Putting It All Together

Creating the Plan

By now you have read about the 10 *Joy of Getting It Done* tools and done all the exercises in each chapter. Or maybe not. Maybe you skipped some of the tools or some of the exercises because they didn't speak to you. There's no rule that says you have to read this book from front to back, or do all of the exercises or use every tool to do it "right." The tools are like clothes in a store – choose the ones that fit and leave the rest behind.

In this chapter, you're going to have the opportunity to create a master plan for each one of the goals that you outlined at the beginning of this book. You'll have a chance to go back and review the applicable exercises and bring everything that you found useful into one place for each goal. Not all of the tools will work for all of your goals, so don't try to force the issue if a tool doesn't seem to fit. There's no "one size fits all" here. It's about what works for you.

New Routines

Choose one from your list on page 6: _____

Which of the 10 tools will you use to establish this routine into your life?

✔	Tool	Page	✔	Tool	Page
	#1: Use a Whole Number	20		#6 – Make It Part of an Existing Routine	59
	#2 – Start Small, Increase Slowly	28		#7 – Deal with Distractions	65
	#3 – Break It Down into Manageable Pieces	N/A		#8 – Reward Yourself	75
	#4 – Make Your Decision Ahead of Time	38		#9 – Avoid Your Personal Black Holes	79
	#5 – Make It a Commitment	44		#10 – Get Support	84

Go back and look at the exercises for each tool that you checked off. Using everything you wrote in each exercise, create a plan for introducing this new routine into your life and write it down here or type up a plan on your computer.

New Routine: _____

_____

_____

_____

_____

_____

_____

_____

_____

_____

_____

_____

_____

_____

_____

_____

_____

_____

_____

_____

_____

Tasks You Avoid

Choose one from your list on page 8: _____

Which of the 10 tools will you use to do this task instead of avoiding it?

✔	Tool	Page	✔	Tool	Page
	#1: Use a Whole Number	20		#6 – Make It Part of an Existing Routine	60
	#2 – Start Small, Increase Slowly	N/A		#7 – Deal with Distractions	66
	#3 – Break It Down into Manageable Pieces	33		#8 – Reward Yourself	75
	#4 – Make Your Decision Ahead of Time	39		#9 – Avoid Your Personal Black Holes	79
	#5 – Make It a Commitment	46		#10 – Get Support	85

Go back and look at the exercises for each tool that you checked off. Using everything you wrote in each exercise, create a plan for doing the task and write it down here or type up a plan on your computer.

_____

_____

_____

_____

_____

_____

_____

_____

_____

Part 3 – Putting It All Together

Overwhelming Projects

Choose one from your list on page 10: _____

Which of the 10 tools will you use to tackle this project?

✔	Tool	Page	✔	Tool	Page
	#1: Use a Whole Number	21		#6 – Make It Part of an Existing Routine	N/A
	#2 – Start Small, Increase Slowly	N/A		#7 – Deal with Distractions	67
	#3 – Break It Down into Manageable Pieces	34		#8 – Reward Yourself	75
	#4 – Make Your Decision Ahead of Time	40		#9 – Avoid Your Personal Black Holes	79
	#5 – Make It a Commitment	50		#10 – Get Support	87

Go back and look at the exercises for each tool that you checked off. Using everything you wrote in each exercise, create a plan for doing this project and write it down here or type up a plan on your computer.

_____

_____

_____

_____

_____

_____

_____

_____

_____

Part 3 – Putting It All Together

You can come up with plans for all of your other goals; just write them on a separate piece of paper or type them into the computer.

But What If...

Now you have your plans in place and are ready to move forward. For some people, this is all that is needed – a structure, a plan of action and some tools to make it all work. But what happens when you start to backslide? Maintenance is often the most difficult part. And what if you are having trouble starting, even if you have a plan? Sometimes you have to look deeper. Maintenance and exploring obstacles are the subjects of the next two chapters of this book.

Part 4
Staying on Course

Maintaining Change

Wе've all heard of yo-yo dieters. Maybe you're one of them. Or maybe you know someone who says, "Quitting smoking is easy – I've done it hundreds of times!"

Maintenance is often the most difficult phase. The excitement of making the change has worn off, as has the euphoria that accompanies reaching a goal. Those who have noticed your change and complimented you on it aren't saying anything anymore. Even if they are, sometimes their encouragement can be depressing as you feel yourself backsliding. Suddenly you feel that people will be disappointed in you, and you start to feel disappointed in yourself, but negative reinforcement rarely gets you back in the saddle. Here are some strategies that might help.

Decrease the Amount

When maintenance becomes a struggle, it can be helpful to scale back for a while, then increase slowly again. Although strength training is now a habit for me, I still occasionally get into a bit of a slump. At those times, I cut back on the number of machines I use, the amount of weight or the number of repetitions. Even if I only work out for 10 or 15 minutes, this keeps me in the routine of going to the Y. Sometimes once I'm there, I do more machines, weight or reps than I intended. But even if I don't do the full amount, I'm at least keeping the momentum going.

Get Support

When you start to slip, positive support is important. Critical support is counterproductive. Shaming you, making you feel guilty and beating up on you are not supportive, as you are probably feeling bad enough. Finding solutions, looking for ways to scale back or cheering you on when you make even a small effort are all things your support people can do to be truly helpful.

Was the Change Right for You?

Examining the change can be useful. Did you make the change because you truly wanted to, or because you caved in to pressure? Were you ready to make the change? Did you do it because someone else did it and you thought it might be good for you? Did you make the change because it was in vogue? These are all good questions to ponder when you are struggling with maintenance.

Is It Maintainable?

One pitfall I've seen when it comes to getting organized is people setting up beautiful, but fussy systems. Everything looks great when it's finished, but it's just not maintainable. It doesn't take much to throw off a system. Consider a lid on a plastic storage box. In order to put something into this box, you have to take the box off its shelf, remove the lid, put the item into the box, close the lid and put the box back – five steps. If there's no convenient place to set the box during this process, the mission is probably doomed. But if there's no lid, you can just throw the item into the box – one step.

Consider how preschool toys are stored. The system is so easy that, well, even a three-year-old can use it! There's a box for blocks, a box for toy vehicles and a box for dress-up clothes. To put something away, all the kids have to do is throw it in the appropriate box. No arranging is necessary. Each box might get a bit messy, but when you look for something, it's narrowed down to one box, and not a whole closet – or room. Frankly, when it comes to cleaning up, most of us revert to being preschoolers. We just won't put things away if it takes a lot of effort, especially if we are in a hurry.

This concept applies to more than just cleaning up. David, who lives in the city, joined a gym that has no parking and is a 15-minute walk from his house. As there were no other gyms available for him to join, we agreed that going to a gym would not be a sustainable option for him for getting in shape, especially when the weather was bad.

Right Change, Wrong Implementation?

Even if you've made the right change, but you've done it in a way that's not right for you, you may be doomed to failure. If you hate the exercise you picked, no matter how good it is supposed to be, you probably won't continue it. If you read a book on time management and struggle to follow the system, it's probably not the right system for you even if it works perfectly for your best friend.

Did you jump in whole-hog, instead of introducing the change slowly? Did you give yourself credit for each bit of progress, no matter how small, or did you berate yourself for not doing more in a shorter time?

Instead of just feeling bad about slipping back, do a little analysis. Drop the "shoulds," as in, "I *should* be able to do this!" I hear that a lot as an ADHD coach. Find out who you are and make changes that work *with* who you are, not against your very nature.

Call In the Pros

If you find you just can't seem to maintain your change on your own, it might be time to call in a professional. This is where coaching can be very helpful. It's the job of a coach to help you ferret out what went wrong, then work with you to come up with a plan that works for you. If you feel that you can't afford to work with a coach, find an accredited coaching school on the International Coach Federation website and contact them. Sometimes coaching schools have students who would be willing to work with you at a reduced rate.

If you're struggling with organization, a good professional organizer might be the place to start. Whether or not you have (or suspect you have) ADHD, a professional organizer who specializes in working with ADHD clients can be highly effective. You don't have to have ADHD to suffer from its symptoms. If getting and staying organized is a constant struggle, an ADHD organization specialist might be just the ticket.

There are lots of other professionals you can hire as well – nutritionists and personal trainers, for example. You might just need a few sessions to get yourself back on track, or you might want ongoing support. Either way, you don't have to go it alone.

But what if you can't even get to the maintenance stage – in fact, you can't seem to get out of the gate on making a change? Then it's time to take a deeper look at what's getting in your way. We'll look at possible obstacles in the next chapter.

Overcoming Obstacles

What happens when systems, plans and structures aren't enough? Maybe you've worked all the way through this book. You've done all of the exercises, and you have a plan. But somehow, you just can't seem to get started. What do you do when your strategy isn't working?

Sometimes when a plan isn't working, it just takes a little tweaking. But if you've tweaked it several times and still nothing is getting accomplished, it's time to look a little deeper.

"We can't solve problems by using the same kind of thinking we used when we created them"[*] Inappropriate or old belief systems get in the way. Or there might be feelings that are going to have to be dealt with before the plan can be executed. There are lots of reasons that people can get stuck. Here are some of them and some suggestions for further reading.

Not Ready to Change

James Prochaska, Ph.D., and his team at the University of Rhode Island found that there are actually six stages of change. These are documented in his book, *Changing for Good*.[1] Here's my summary of the stages:

- **Precontemplation** – At this stage you have no awareness of a need to change, or no intention of making a change that others are urging you to make. You might be in denial ("My grandfather smoked until he was 97 years old"), you might be resistant, or the change might be completely off of your radar.
- **Contemplation** – You know that you might like to make a change someday, but not now.
- **Preparation** – You've decided that you want to change soon, and you are getting ready to do so. You are finding resources and creating an approach. You are probably in this stage if you are reading this book.

---

[*] Attributed to Albert Einstein

- **Action** – This is the stage when the change actually takes place.
- **Maintenance** – Probably the hardest stage; this is where people typically fall off the wagon, gain back the weight, quit exercising, etc. This stage was explored more deeply in the previous chapter.
- **Termination** – The change has become such a part of your life that you no longer think about it, and you just maintain it automatically. It can take a good six months to a year or longer to reach the termination stage. Some people never actually "terminate" but that doesn't mean that they can't succeed. Some people will stay in the Maintenance stage, and will need to be vigilant about not slipping back. Many alcoholics who maintain their sobriety fall into this category.

What Prochaska learned was that if you try to change before you are ready, or you were pressured or brow-beaten into changing, your chance of success is low. Understanding what stage you are in, and not trying to change prematurely, are important if you want to maximize your chances for success.

Boundary Issues

It's not unusual for clients to tell me that they can't get to their own plans because other people keep asking them to do things, and they can't say no. Sometimes it's a bad case of the "disease to please" and sometimes it's just because people don't have the language or the skills to say no. Some people have been raised with the notion that saying no is selfish. And still others find themselves enjoying being a rescuer – it gives them a good feeling, but at quite a cost to them and their families.

If you find it hard to say no to people, I highly recommend the book, *When I Say No, I Feel Guilty*[2] by Manuel Smith, Ph.D. Perennial wisdom for over 30 years, its message is as useful and relevant today as it was the day it was written.

Not Knowing Your Own Style

Although this can pertain to anyone, I find it especially true for my ADHD clients. Well-meaning friends will tell you what worked for them, and you assume it must be right for you also. When it doesn't work you assume the problem is you, not the system, the change or the solution you are trying to implement. You don't have to listen to your friends to make this mistake; society sends strong messages about how certain things *should* be done.

Linda Roggli, who has ADHD, became a lot more successful and happy in her life when she stopped trying to accomplish her goals in the standard and accepted way and started following her own quirky, but effective (for her) style. She documented her journey in her book,

Confessions of an ADDiva.[3] Whether or not you struggle with the symptoms of ADHD, her off-beat and highly personal approach to life is an inspiring read, and can help give readers permission to follow their own paths. You can find the book through her website, *www.addiva.net.*

Facing the Feelings

Sometimes the biggest obstacle to achieving your goals is facing the feelings that will come up for you when you begin to execute your plan. Those feelings can be lying just under the surface and you don't even realize that they are there, but you subconsciously avoid working on your goal because, on some level, you know those feelings are going to surface when you get started. Shame, indecision, anger and sadness are just a few of the feelings that can keep us stuck, and we might not even realize we have them.

When clients are stuck, sometimes I'll ask them to close their eyes and imagine that they are just about to start executing their plan. Then I ask them what feelings are coming up for them. Rob wanted to clean up his work room so he'd have a place for his hobbies, but no matter how many times we modified the plan to deal with it, he never even started it. I asked him to close his eyes and imagine he was standing in the doorway of the room, and asked him what he was feeling. He was quiet for a few minutes, and then he said that the room was always uncomfortably cold. In addition, he knew he needed to get rid of a lot of stuff that he'd wasted money on and never used. He felt some shame around the waste. Finally, he identified some anger he had towards one of the members of his family about the way the room had been set up.

We were able to talk about each of these issues. By just naming the feelings and talking about them, it took away some of their power. It also prepared him to experience the feelings, so he wasn't blindsided by them when he started working on the room. We re-framed the concept of the wasted money by looking for a charity to whom he could donate the unused items. By finding someone who could use them, the money was no longer a waste, but a gift to people who were less fortunate. When we talked the next week, the room was done.

If you think that feelings are getting in the way of your progress, writing about them is one way to uncover and face them. Talking to a trusted friend, clergy member, psychotherapist or life coach can also help you find out what's keeping you stuck.

Acquiring Stuff

When I give my presentation, I say to my audience, "Raise your hand if you need more stuff." This is usually met with chuckles and knowing nods of the head, as people think about how much stuff they own. Most of us have just too much of it. It gets in our way, and it slows us down when we're looking for something. We have to dust it, store it, organize it and move it out of the way. It's a huge impediment to getting things done.

Besides killing the quality of our lives, our stuff is also killing the planet. It takes energy and resources to manufacture and ship, and most of it ends up in a landfill or an incinerator.

Stuff costs us in many ways – money, time, energy. It's taking over our houses, our offices, our desks and our lives. If you have it, you have to manage it. You have to find a place to keep it, or else it gets in your way. If it's out on the counter and doesn't belong there, you have to put back. Unfortunately, all too often the place it "belongs" is the counter because it doesn't really have a home.

At the end of its useful life (if, indeed, there was a useful life), we have to decide if we want to keep or get rid of it. If we decide to get rid of it, then we have to decide how we're going to get rid of it – toss it? sell it? donate it? It all gets quite exhausting.

I've found the best way to deal with stuff is not to acquire it in the first place. That's easier said than done. We're hunter-gatherers by nature; it's fun to acquire stuff! But if it doesn't come into your life, you don't have to worry about it. Really, how much of the stuff that we own is useful or brings us pleasure? And how do we keep the rest of it out of our lives?

The Christmas Tree Shops jingle reminds us, "Don't you just love a bargain?" They know how hard it is to resist something that's really cute or really inexpensive or both. They, and all the other retailers out there, strategically place products to promote impulse buying. They advertise items that are enticing. They appeal to the hunter-gatherer part of us that is in our genetic code, and they do a good job.

Do you go to the store only to get items that you know you need? Or do you shop as a form of recreation? If it's the latter, you probably have way too much stuff in your life. How about catalogs? Do you love to look through them? If so, how often do you end up buying things you don't need, things that seem like a good idea at the time, but that really just use up your money, space and time?

If you go to a conference, do you gather all of the freebies that the vendors offer you? How often do they end up on that ever-growing pile of things you are going to get to – eventually?

The next time you have that cute little bargain in your hands at the store, or you find that very useful-appearing item in a catalog, or you scoop up all of the free handouts anywhere, ask yourself the following questions:

- Where will I keep this once I get it home?
- When and how often will I actually use it?
- Where will it be in a week? a month? a year?
- What will ultimately happen to it?

If you only use it once, it will end up cluttering your house until you eventually toss it. It's far easier to walk away without it than have to deal with it in your space.

Just before I pass out my own handouts at the end of my presentation, I ask people to consider these questions, and then decide if they will really use the handouts. Once, after I gave my talk at a local library, a woman came up to me with her hands full of items, not just my own handouts but ones that the library was also giving away. She said to me, "I want you to know that you really made an impression on me. I was going to take all of these home, but I've decided not to." Smiling, she dumped the whole pile on the table in front of me and walked away. She doesn't know it, but she made my day.

Parting Thoughts

Writing this book definitely qualified as an overwhelming project for me. I used a lot of the *Getting It Done* tools to make it through, adapting them to suit my needs for this particular task. Here are the ones that I used, and how I used them:

Tool #1: Use a Whole Number – I pretty much wrote this entire book in 20-minute chunks. Even on those days when I wrote for hours, it was always with the timer going. In addition, I had a pile of pennies on my desk, and every time the timer buzzed, I moved a penny from one pile to the other and reset the timer. At the end of the day, I counted the pennies and recorded the time in my calendar. What will I do with that information? Probably nothing. But it was fun seeing the pennies pile up each day, and satisfying to write down the time. I'm not sure it really matters why.

Tool #3: Break It Down into Manageable Pieces –That's what my timer did for me. Although I had the framework of the entire book in my mind, I found it easier just to keep pluggin' away at it without thinking about the whole thing. Otherwise, I would have been completely overwhelmed. It really was a case of putting one foot in front of the other until I got to the end.

Tool #4: Make Your Decision Ahead of Time – It wasn't always easy to sit down and start writing, especially if I hadn't worked on the book for a few days. So I tried to decide the day before if the next day was going to be a writing day and, if so, make some decision as to when I was going to get started on it.

Tool #5: Make It a Commitment – Writing this book was a calling. I really felt that I didn't have a choice; I just knew I was going to do it. I had a deep commitment to myself to finish it, and it never occurred to me that I wouldn't see it through. I decided not to make a declaration to anyone about it, as I didn't feel like I wanted or needed to. I just followed my heart.

At one point as I neared the end, I found I was neglecting other duties, but it was hard to stop writing long enough to attend to them. So I sent an email to a couple of friends committing not to work on the book until I completed a list of things that really needed to be done. That was a huge help. I finished the list, which also gave me a much-needed break from writing.

Then I emailed my friends and told them I had followed through. I returned to the book the next day feeling much more calm and refreshed.

Tool #7: Deal with Distractions – This turned out not to be much of a problem until the very end, when I started feeling a bit burned out. There were times that I did allow myself to be distracted by things that were not urgent, but each time I stopped the timer, quickly dealt with the distraction, then started the timer again and got back to work. There were other times I didn't allow myself to be distracted for any reason until the timer buzzed. I made good progress, so I didn't worry too much about about being strict on this one until I got to the end of the project. At that point, I needed to be strict with myself because I was having trouble staying focused. When that started happening, I made a decision about how I was going to deal with distractions before I started working.

Tool #8: Reward Yourself – I found the process of creating this book pretty rewarding in itself, but there were times that I threw in little Premack reinforcers when I got bogged down, like, "I'm not going to clean up the kitchen until I've worked for an hour." I hate clutter, so cleaning up is a high probability activity for me. Also, cleaning up the kitchen gave me a break from sitting at my desk after doing a chunk of work.

I'm telling you how I used the tools because I want to encourage you to use them as you see fit. Adapt them to fit your style. Or use them exactly as presented if that's better for you. Just don't let them become a "should," a burden or something else to feel bad about. They are tools, not rules. If they don't enhance your life, then don't use them.

As I conclude this book, I can only hope that it's been useful to you. Maybe you already knew some of this stuff, or made up some similar tools of your own to get things done. If so, this book might have been validating for you.

Hopefully you realized that you are not alone. There are lots of people, including me, who struggle with getting things done. Overall, I've gotten pretty good at it, but I've been using these tools for a lot of years. I developed them over the course of my life because I needed them. I based many of them on what I learned in classes I've taken, workshops I've attended and books I've read, but many others I created on the fly just because I needed them at the time. Using them, I have my time under control and my space organized – most of the time!

Sometimes, however, the most important thing in life is not getting things done. I often have to remind myself that we are human *beings*, not human *doings*. Although getting things done is important, and even a joy, not getting things done can also be a joy. I'm talking about taking time to appreciate and be grateful for all we have, for our world, for the gift of life itself. Maybe that's the best thing to *do* that there is.

Appendix
The Questionnaires

Looking at Your Life

These questionnaires were originally created to help me gain a better understanding of my clients and their challenges. However, my clients often report that the process of filling them out is a useful and thought-provoking exercise.

Completing some or all of the following questionnaires prior to beginning *The Joy of Getting It Done* can be very helpful as you set goals for the program.

There are a lot of questionnaires. Don't be intimidated by the number of pages, and don't feel that you have to do them all. They are mostly multiple choice, so it should not take you a long time to complete any of them. Some of them may be extremely helpful to you, others not so much. Use them as you see fit, modify the questions and add your own. Pick the closest answers, or modify or make up answers if none of the choices work for you.

There's no score to be tallied; the goal is to give you a bird's-eye view of your overall life management. It's up to you to decide if what you are doing works for you. There are no right or wrong answers. I intentionally tried to make this easy and fun to do.

The questionnaires address time, stuff, space and information management, for both your personal life and your professional life. In addition, the personal questionnaires also take a look at your wellness habits, financial picture and management of your life's logistics – those nuts and bolts things like laundry and meals that need attention.

If you are going through the questionnaires before starting *The Joy of Getting It Done*, they might help you set your objectives. If you would like to do them again at another time to track your progress, you can print out additional copies from my website at *www.JoyofGTD.com/Questionnaires*.

Your Personal Time

I usually watch television (focused watching, not having it on in the background):

___ Rarely.

___ Less than an hour per day.

___ More than an hour per day.

___ More than 2 hours per day.

___ More than 3 hours per day.

I waste time on the computer:

___ Rarely.

___ Less than an hour per day.

___ More than an hour per day.

___ More than 2 hours per day.

___ More than 3 hours per day.

Overall, on a scale of 1-10 where
1 = "I generally use my cell phone only for emergency and essential phone calls," and
10 = "I tend to text or talk on my cell every free minute I have,"

I would give myself a rating of: ____.

The state of the overall organization of my house:

___ Is not a problem.

___ Makes accomplishing things take longer than it should.

___ Really causes me to waste a lot of time.

When looking for something that I use regularly:

___ I can usually locate it immediately.

___ I can usually find it fairly quickly.

___ It takes me a while but I find it eventually.

___ I often have to give up.

When looking for something that I use occasionally:

___ I can usually locate it immediately.

___ I can usually find it fairly quickly.

___ It takes me a while but I find it eventually.

___ I often have to give up.

When it comes to controlling my little corner of the world, I:

___ Try to live responsibly, but accept that there are things I can't control.

___ Probably try to control more than is realistic.

___ Am a complete control freak.

___ Other: _____.

I tend to be:

___ Pretty relaxed about things.

___ A little obsessive, but not enough that it's a problem.

___ Somewhat obsessive about things.

___ Obsessive to the point where it truly interferes with my life.

When asked to do something optional that I don't want or have time to do, I:

___ Almost always say no.

___ Usually say no.

___ Sometimes say no.

___ Usually say yes.

___ Almost always say yes.

My volunteer activities are:

___ Mostly things I enjoy and have time to do.

___ Obligations that I need to fulfill and have the time to do.

___ Obligations that I need to fulfill but don't have the time to do.

___ Things I don't have time for and don't have obligations to fulfill but I can't say no.

Overall, on a scale of 1-10 where
1 = "My brain gets regular downtime (no cell phone, computer, TV, etc.)," and
10 = "My brain is plugged into something every waking minute,"

I would give myself a rating of: _____.

I take time for leisure activities:

___ At least once a week.

___ A couple of times a month.

___ Rarely.

___ Yeah, right. Who has time for fun?

If employed, I usually:

___ Take the vacation time that is coming to me.

___ Take most of my vacation time.

___ Do not use all of my vacation time.

The last time I took time off work for vacation or other leisure activity was:

_____.

I take time for activities that nurture me (massage, meditation, hot bath, etc.):

___ At least once per week.

___ At least once per month.

___ Rarely.

___ Never.

For fun and relaxation I: (check all that apply)

___ Watch television.

___ Read.

___ Participate in something physical.

___ Am on a sports team.

___ Go out to dinner with friends or family.

___ Go to movies, plays or concerts.

___ Do crafts, play an instrument or sing.

___ Journal, write poetry, etc.

___ Garden.

___ Other:_____.

If I had more time, I would:

___ Watch television.

___ Read.

___ Participate in something physical.

___ Join a sports team.

___ Go out to dinner with friends or family.

___ Go to movies, plays or concerts.

___ Do crafts, play an instrument or sing.

___ Journal, write poetry, etc.

___ Garden.

___ Other:_____.

Overall, on a scale of 1-10 where
1 = "I regularly take time for recreating (read: 're-creating')," and
10 = "I never take time to relax or have fun,"

I would give myself a rating of: _____.

Overall, on a scale of 1-10 where
1 = "My personal time is pretty calm and in control," and
10 = "My personal time is hopelessly frenetic,"

I would give myself a rating of: _____.

What priority level would you give to making changes to your personal time management?

___ High priority   ___ Medium priority   ___ Low priority

Your Personal Stuff and Space

Rate the following according to this scale:

> 1 = Usually neat, clean and well organized
> 2 = A bit cluttered; I can usually find things pretty easily
> 3 = Medium cluttered; I could definitely use some help
> 4 = Pretty messy; finding things is pretty difficult
> 5 = In danger of being declared a federal disaster area

	1	2	3	4	5	N/A
Bedroom closet, dresser, other bedroom storage						
Bedroom horizontal surfaces						
Car						
Kitchen counters						
Kitchen cupboards						
Garage						
Basement						
Attic						
Purse/wallet						
Other household storage						
Most horizontal surfaces (including the floor)						
Other:						

I have the following in my home awaiting my attention: (check all that apply)

____ Stacks of miscellaneous stuff that have been there for ages

____ Clothes that no longer fit or are no longer in style or that I just don't wear

____ Shoes I haven't worn for ages

____ Clothes that need to be mended

____ Broken items that I'm going to get around to repairing or having repaired

____ Old sports equipment, hobby supplies, etc. that I no longer use

____ Toys that my children have grown out of

____ Other: _____

When it comes to putting away my stuff:

___ Everything has a place.

___ Most things have a place.

___ There's a fair amount that sits out because it doesn't have a place.

___ There's a large amount that sits out because it doesn't have a place.

The main reason that things in my house don't have a place is because:

___ I don't have enough space.

___ I have enough space; I just never got around to assigning them a place.

___ N/A, most things in my house have a place.

How easy/difficult is it to tidy up your house?

___ Pretty easy

___ Not too difficult, maybe a little challenging

___ Pretty difficult, usually stuff just gets tossed out of sight

___ Impossible, too much stuff, not enough storage, no organization

When I go to a place that is giving away freebies, I usually:

___ Take everything; I can't resist anything that's free whether I need it or not.

___ Take more than I think I'll use, and often don't use most of it.

___ Take only what I think I'll use, and often don't use most of it.

___ Take only what I think I'll use, and usually use what I take.

How often do you end up purchasing something new because you can't find the one that you already own?

___ Never or rarely

___ Occasionally

___ Often

How long would it take to find:	Under 10 Seconds	Probably a Minute or Two	It Would Take a While
A pen that writes			
A pencil that is sharpened or has lead			
A stapler			
A working flashlight			
A spare key for your house			
Other:			

When I replace a piece of electronic equipment (computer, mp3 player, camera, etc.), I:

___ Get rid of the old one.

___ Usually get rid of the old one, but sometimes keep it just in case.

___ Have an electronic graveyard in my basement.

When the kids bring home projects, artwork, homework papers, etc., I:

___ Keep every one or most of them.

___ Keep only the best or most special ones.

___ Toss all of them.

___ Other: _____.

___ N/A, I don't have kids.

When it comes to memorabilia, birthday cards, notes, souvenirs, I:

___ Keep them all.

___ Keep most of them.

___ Keep a few of the most special but get rid of the rest.

___ Toss all of them.

Overall, on a scale of 1-10 where

1 = "I get rid of everything I don't use and keep nothing out of sentiment," and
10 = "I keep everything; I could probably be on that TV show about hoarders,"

I would give myself a rating of: _____.

Overall, on a scale of 1-10 where

1 = "I work very hard not to acquire any more more stuff in my life," and
10 = "I just love to shop, receive gifts, get free stuff, and generally acquire anything and everything,"

I would give myself a rating of: _____.

Overall, on a scale of 1-10 where

1 = "My personal stuff and space are completely under control," and
10 = "My personal stuff and space are completely out of control,"

I would give myself a rating of: _____.

What priority level would you give making changes to your personal stuff and space issues?

___ High priority   ___ Medium priority   ___ Low priority

Your Personal Information Management

My to-do list is:

___ Organized, all in one or two places.

___ On little notes all over the place.

___ Non-existent.

I have the following piles in my home awaiting my attention: (check all that apply)

___ Magazines and other personal reading

___ Non-junk mail that I'm going to get to eventually

___ Junk mail and catalogs I want to go through

___ Paper that needs to be filed, recycled or otherwise dealt with

___ Other: _____

Regarding junk mail: (check all that apply)

___ I get a lot.

___ I get a little.

___ Junk mail slows me down when I go through my mail each day.

___ Junk mail does not take up much of my time.

___ Junk mail is adding significantly to the clutter in my house.

___ Junk mail is not a clutter problem for me.

___ I have opted out of junk mail at websites like *www.catalogchoice.org* or *www.DMAchoice.org.*

___ When I get an unwanted catalog, I go to the company's website and opt out of their mailing list.

What do you do with junk mail that comes to your home?

___ Save most of it to look at sometime

___ Recycle most of it immediately

___ Read what is useful in a timely fashion, recycle the rest

___ Other: _____

Which most closely describes your magazine, newspaper and other personal subscriptions?

___ I have subscriptions I know I'll never read.

___ I have subscriptions I plan to eventually read.

___ I usually read all of the periodicals I subscribe to before the next one comes.

___ I don't have any subscriptions.

My file drawers are: (check all that apply)

___ Mostly organized.

___ Mostly disorganized.

___ Full of stuff that I'll probably never need again.

___ Filled with files I might need but rarely use that are taking up prime filing space instead of being archived elsewhere.

___ A total disaster.

___ Not full and have space for additional filing.

___ Jammed full.

The information I have on my personal computer is:

___ Extremely important.

___ Pretty important.

___ Somewhat important.

___ Not at all important.

My passwords for my computer accounts are: (check all that apply)

___ The same for each account.

___ Different for each account.

___ The same for some accounts but a lot are different for other accounts.

___ Something simple to guess like my first name.

___ Trickier to guess, but not as secure as they could be.

___ A combination of upper and lower case letters, numbers and symbols.

I back up my computer files:

___ Daily or more often.

___ At least once a week.

___ At least once a month.

___ Never.

Regarding email: (check all that apply)

___ I check out every email that comes into my email box, including junk mail, jokes, etc.

___ I usually quickly delete spam, jokes, etc. without reading.

___ I have a good spam filter.

___ I spend about the right amount of time on my email.

___ I spend too much time on my email.

___ My email time is way out of control.

Regarding paper:

___ My paper is under control.

___ My paper is somewhat out of control.

___ Help! I'm buried in paper!

Do you know where the following are?	Definitely Know	Probably Know	No Clue	N/A
Receipts to items still under warranty				
Your homeowner's insurance policy				
Manuals to appliances and other items				
Your doctor's phone number (other than in the phone book)				
Your health insurance card				
Your birth certificate				
Your child(ren)'s last medical checkup record				

Where are your important documents (deed, car title, marriage license, birth certificate, etc.)?

___ Safely stored in a safe deposit box at the bank or in a fireproof container at home

___ In my desk drawer or other location well-known to me

___ In a location that I'm pretty sure I could find within about 15 minutes

___ I don't have a clue; they must be somewhere!

The business cards that people give me are:

___ All over the place.

___ In one specific place, but not sorted.

___ Sorted and filed or scanned into the computer.

___ Other: _____.

When I go to a meeting, class or convention (like a home show), I usually:

___ Take a bunch of handouts but never look at them.

___ Take a bunch of handouts, look them over and discard the ones I don't want.

___ Take a bunch of handouts and read them all.

___ Take a few handouts and read the ones that I take.

___ Take a few handouts but usually don't get to them.

Overall, on a scale of 1-10 where
1 = "My personal information is completely under control," and
10 = "My personal information is completely out of control,"

I would give myself a rating of: _____.

What priority level would you give to making changes to your personal information management?

___ High priority   ___ Medium priority   ___ Low priority

Your Life Logistics

I do my laundry:

____ On a regular basis.

____ When I'm close to being out of clothes.

____ When I'm completely out of clothes and desperate.

____ Someone else is in charge of my laundry.

I pick up/drop off my dry cleaning:

____ On a regular basis.

____ When I have something to be cleaned, but then I get it done.

____ When I'm desperate.

____ Clothes that need to be dry cleaned often never get worn again.

____ I have little or no dry cleaning.

For dinner, I usually:

____ Eat a healthy, home-cooked dinner.

____ Thaw a frozen dinner or other store-bought food.

____ Do take-out or go out.

____ Grab whatever I can on the fly.

If I live with my family, we:

____ Usually sit down and eat together.

____ Sometimes sit down and eat together.

____ Rarely sit down and eat together.

____ N/A, I don't live with family members.

Who's in charge of planning/preparing your food?

____ I'm in charge of planning/preparing my food.

____ Someone else in my household is in charge of food.

____ I share the responsibility with someone.

Who is in charge of buying groceries?

___ I'm in charge of the grocery shopping.

___ Someone else does it.

___ I share the grocery shopping.

Check off all that apply to your household's grocery shopping:

___ Shopping is done frequently, as things are needed.

___ A large shopping trip is done every week or two, filling in as needed in between.

___ No one gets around to it regularly so I often end up doing take-out or going out to dinner.

Regarding meal planning:

___ I plan meals ahead of time and shop accordingly.

___ I tend to plan meals the day of the meal, and it works pretty well.

___ I tend to plan meals the day of the meal, and it's not working very well.

___ Meal planning, are you *kidding*?

House repair/upkeep: (check all that apply)

___ I live in an apartment so don't have to worry about repairs.

___ Home repairs are done (or repair people are called) when problems first appear.

___ Home repairs are generally done when problems get really bad.

___ Home repairs generally don't get done.

What do you do about household cleaning? (check all that apply)

___ I have a cleaning service.

___ Another family member does it.

___ I do it (or share it) regularly.

___ It gets done occasionally.

___ It gets done when the dirt could support industrial agriculture.

___ It never gets done.

What is the plan for tidying up your house?

___ It never really gets tidied up.

___ It gets done occasionally.

___ It gets done regularly; it's usually pretty neat.

Who's in charge of keeping the house in order?

___ Someone else does it.

___ It's my job to keep the house in order.

___ I share the responsibility.

What do you do about yard upkeep? (check all that apply)

___ I don't have a yard.

___ I hire services to deal with the mowing, leaves, snow removal, etc.

___ Another family member does it.

___ I do it (or share it) regularly.

___ It gets done occasionally.

___ It doesn't get done.

Car repair/upkeep: (check all that apply)

___ I don't have a car.

___ I have a car, but someone else is in charge of maintenance.

___ I usually do my state inspection after it has expired.

___ I usually do my state inspection the day before or the day it expires.

___ I usually do my state inspection several days or more before it expires.

___ I have the oil changed every 3,000-5,000 miles.

___ I have the oil changed every 5,000-10,000 miles.

___ I often drive more than 10,000 miles before I change the oil.

___ Car repairs and maintenance are done in a timely fashion.

___ Car repairs are done when the car won't go anymore.

Regarding library items/video rentals:

___ I don't borrow library items or rent videos.

___ I usually return my library items or videos on time.

___ I often return my library items or videos late.

___ It's not unusual for me to lose a library item or video and have to pay for it.

I have the following in place: (check all that apply)

___ A will

___ A durable power of attorney

___ A health care proxy

___ A living will

Overall, on a scale of 1-10 where
1 = "My life logistics are working really well," and
10 = "My life logistics are a disaster,"

I would give myself a rating of: _____.

What priority level would you give to making changes to your life logistics?

___ High priority   ___ Medium priority   ___ Low priority

Your Personal Wellness

Sleep

How much sleep do you generally get on weeknights?

___ Less than 4 hours

___ 4-5 hours

___ 6-7 hours

___ 7 or more hours

How much sleep do you generally get on weekend nights?

___ Less than 4 hours

___ 4-5 hours

___ 6-7 hours

___ 7 or more hours

Do you usually go to bed at the same time each night?

___ No, it often varies.

___ Yes, on weekdays, but I stay up later on weekends and sleep in.

___ Yes, but I wake up at a different time on weekends vs. weekdays.

___ Yes, I go to bed close to the same time every night and get up close to the same time every morning (give or take an hour).

How long does it usually take you to fall asleep after you turn off the lights?

___ Less than 15 minutes

___ 15-30 minutes

___ More than 30 minutes

How often do you usually wake up in the middle of the night?

___ Never

___ 1-2 times

___ 3 or more times

When I wake up in the middle of the night, I:

___ Generally get back to sleep quickly.

___ Lie awake for 20 minutes or more.

___ Get out of bed if I can't get back to sleep.

I watch television/use the computer within 2 hours of bedtime:

___ Often.

___ Occasionally.

___ Rarely.

___ Never.

I watch television/use the computer in my bedroom:

___ Often.

___ Occasionally.

___ Rarely.

___ Never.

I have an alcoholic drink within 3 hours of bedtime:

___ Often.

___ Occasionally.

___ Rarely.

___ Never.

I intentionally nap (as opposed to nodding off):

___ Often.

___ Occasionally.

___ Rarely.

___ Never.

I nod off during the day:

___ Often.

___ Occasionally.

___ Rarely.

___ Never.

Regarding my tiredness level during the day:

___ I'm really tired; I often have a hard time making it through the day.

___ I'm generally tired but functioning.

___ I'm sometimes tired; it's not a problem overall.

___ I'm rarely tired; I feel rested in general.

Physical Fitness

I usually do cardio exercise:

___ Regularly, ___ times per week.

___ Occasionally.

___ Rarely or never.

I usually do strength training:

___ Regularly, ___ times per week.

___ Occasionally.

___ Rarely or never.

I usually do stretching exercises:

___ Regularly, ___ times per week.

___ Occasionally.

___ Rarely or never.

Eating Habits

Please check all that apply to you:

___ I tend to eat a fair amount of processed and prepared foods.

___ I eat out a lot or do a lot of take-out.

___ I drink a lot of soda (either diet or regular).

___ I drink a lot of coffee (more than 2 cups/day).

___ I eat a lot of high-fat foods.

___ I eat a lot of sugary foods.

___ I tend to grab whatever is handy to eat.

___ I usually skip breakfast or just have a cup of coffee.

___ I eat something sweet and/or highly processed for breakfast.

___ I eat a lot of fresh vegetables and fruits.

___ I tend to eat whole grains.

___ Most of what I eat is prepared from scratch.

___ I try to drink water to stay hydrated throughout the day.

___ I take vitamins, minerals and other supplements.

___ I eat a good breakfast.

Overall, I'd say my diet and eating habits are:

___ Very healthy.

___ Pretty healthy.

___ Fair.

___ Pretty unhealthy.

___ Terrible.

Other

The last time I had a checkup, my doctor told me to: (check all that apply)

___ Lose weight.

___ Stop smoking.

___ Lower my alcohol intake.

___ Lower my caffeine intake.

___ Lower my sodium intake.

___ Exercise more.

___ Lower my stress level.

___ Change my diet in some way (specify): _____.

___ Other: _____.

___ I haven't had a checkup in years.

Regarding a colonoscopy:

___ I'm under 50.

___ I'm over 50 but up-to-date.

___ I'm over 50 and overdue.

How often do you have a physical?

___ Every year

___ Every two years

___ Rarely

___ Never

How often do you see the dentist?

___ Once a year

___ Twice a year

___ Rarely

___ Never

I have an eye examination:

___ Every year.

___ Every two years.

___ Rarely.

___ Never.

Women over 40: Do you have a yearly mammogram?

___ Yes

___ No

Women: Do you have a yearly gynecological checkup?

___ Yes

___ No

Overall, on a scale of 1-10 where
1 = "I live a very healthy lifestyle," and
10 = "I live a very unhealthy lifestyle,"

I would give myself a rating of: _____.

Overall, on a scale of 1-10 where
1 = "I feel great most of the time," and
10 = "I feel terrible most of the time,"

I would give myself a rating of: _____.

What priority level would you give to making changes to your personal wellness practices?

___ High priority   ___ Medium priority   ___ Low priority

Your Personal Finances

Which of these best describes your overall financial life:

____ I'm going further into debt each day.

____ My current expenses outweigh my income, but I have savings to fall back on so I'm not incurring more debt.

____ I live from paycheck to paycheck, but I break even.

____ I am able to live within my income and put money aside in savings.

____ Other: _____.

Which of these best describes your credit card situation?

____ I don't have credit cards.

____ I pay off my full balance each month on all of my credit cards.

____ I have some credit card debt.

____ I have significant credit card debt.

   Amount of significant debt: $_____ Interest rate: _____%

____ Other: _____.

Which of these is most similar to your debt payment habits?

____ I pay off all of my debts in full every month (except for mortgage and car debt).

____ I pay more than the minimum payment on at least some of my bills every month.

____ I pay the minimum payment on all of my bills every month.

____ Sometimes I can't make the minimum payment on all of my bills every month.

Regarding paying my bills:

____ I pay them manually (by check or online), but on time pretty much every month.

____ I'm sometimes late paying a bill.

____ I often pay bills late.

If so it's because: ____ I forget.   ____ I don't have the money.   ____ Other: _____.

____ I've set up automatic payments for most of my bills.

Which of these describes your savings? (check all that apply)

___ I have no savings or very little savings.

___ I have 6 months of liquid savings available in case of an unforeseen crisis.

___ I have an appropriate (for my age) amount of retirement savings set aside.

___ I am saving for my children's college education.

___ Other: _____

Which of these best describes your shopping? (check all that apply)

___ I make a list and only buy what I planned on or what I need.

___ I try to take advantage of sales for items that I regularly use.

___ I shop for recreation.

___ I tend to do retail therapy if I'm feeling bad.

___ I just can't resist a bargain or something cute, even if I don't need it.

___ I buy things I can't afford right now with credit.

___ I finance expensive luxury items (vacations, etc.) that I can't afford.

___ I have too much stuff because of my buying habits.

___ My buying habits have caused me at least some financial distress.

___ I never return items I change my mind about because it's too much trouble or I can't find the receipt.

___ I have a hard time saying no to myself when it comes to things I want.

___ Other: _____

Which of these best describes your car-buying habits?

___ I pay cash for my car and replace it every ___ years.

___ I pay cash for my car and keep it until it really starts to fall apart.

___ I finance my car and replace it as soon as it's paid off.

___ I finance my car and replace it every 2-3 years.

___ I finance my car and keep it after it's paid off.

___ Other: _____.

I usually prepare my taxes (or have them prepared):

___ Before they are due.

___ At the last minute; it's always a panic.

___ Late; I file for an extension.

___ Late, without filing for an extension.

Regarding late payments:

___ I often pay a penalty.

___ I never pay a penalty.

Regarding my financial organization: (check all that apply)

___ Tax time is awful because I don't keep good records.

___ I can never find receipts when I need them for returning an item or claiming a warranty repair.

___ I'm in charge of keeping track of the finances in my family.

___ I have an accountant or family member who does all of the finances.

___ I share the financial tasks with another family member.

___ I keep my finances on my computer.

___ I balance my checkbook each month.

___ I generally know how much is in my bank accounts at any given time.

___ I have a budget and generally keep within it.

___ I have (or can easily look up) a pretty good idea of how much I spend on different categories such as clothing, take-out, entertainment, etc.

Which of these statements applies most to you?

___ I spend too much money eating out or doing take-out because I'm stuck.

___ I eat out or do take-out occasionally if I'm stuck.

___ I generally only eat out or do take-out because it's fun, not because I'm stuck.

Overall, on a scale of 1-10 where
1 = "My personal finances are very well organized," and
10 = "My personal finances are very disorganized,"

I would give myself a rating of: _____ .

Overall, on a scale of 1-10 where
1 = "My overall financial picture is very secure," and
10 = "My overall financial picture is very insecure,"

I would give myself a rating of: _____ .

What priority level would you give to making changes to your personal financial management?

___ High priority   ___ Medium priority   ___ Low priority

Your Professional Time

Section 1

The questions in this section are for professionals who work in a location *outside of their home*. If you work *from home*, skip to *Section 2*.

The time between when I get up in the morning and when I leave the house is:

____ Relaxed, organized, not stressful.

____ A bit hurried, but I usually get out on time.

____ Fairly crazy; I'm late a lot.

____ A race with the clock; I usually lose.

I usually arrive at work:

____ Relaxed, organized, ready-to-go.

____ A little harried, but not too bad.

____ Pretty frazzled, and then I have a whole day of work ahead of me!

When I first arrive at work:

____ I immediately get distracted by others.

____ I immediately get distracted on my own.

____ I get right to work on the most appropriate task.

____ I get right to work, but usually not on the task I should be doing first.

When I get to work, I start first on:

____ Checking my email.

____ Organizing my day.

____ The most urgent task.

____ The hardest task.

____ The easiest task.

____ Whatever catches my eye first.

____ I usually get grabbed by someone the minute I walk in the door.

____ Other: _____.

I take work home:

___ Often.

___ Occasionally.

___ Rarely.

Section 2

The questions in this section are for people who work *from home*. If you work *outside of your home*, skip to *Section 3*.

When it's time to get started on work, I find that I:

___ Get right to it.

___ Sometimes have a hard time getting to it.

___ Often find that there is something that distracts me from sitting down to work.

___ Getting started working is a frequent and serious problem for me.

Because I live at my workplace:

___ I never seem to get away from my job; there are no boundaries between my personal life and my professional life.

___ Sometimes the boundaries between job and home are a bit blurred, but not always.

___ I'm pretty good at separating my work life and home life.

When I begin my workday, I start first on:

___ Checking my email.

___ Organizing my day.

___ The most urgent task.

___ The hardest task.

___ The easiest task.

___ Whatever catches my eye first.

___ Other: _____.

When I start working in the morning, I:

___ Get right to work on the most appropriate task.

___ Get right to work, but usually not on the task I should be doing first.

Section 3

The questions in this section are for all professionals.

When I leave work, or finish for the day, my desk is usually:

___ Cleared off or at least tidy.

___ A disaster.

___ Something in between.

I generally do things that need to be done:

___ When they become urgent.

___ When I'm in the right mood or it feels like the right time; it works well for me.

___ When I'm in the right mood or it feels like the right time, but it doesn't work well.

___ I plan ahead and get them done in a timely fashion.

When my boss or a customer asks me to do an optional task that I don't want to do or don't have time for, I:

___ Say yes anyway, but then don't do it or only do it partway.

___ Say yes anyway, and do it well.

___ Generally say no unless I think it is really important that I say yes.

___ Say no to everything I don't have the time to do.

When asked by a peer to do something that is not my job, I usually:

___ Weigh the situation first, including my workload, then say yes if appropriate.

___ Say yes most of the time, even if I don't have time.

___ Sometimes say yes, even if I don't have time.

___ Just say no.

I delegate tasks that are appropriate to be delegated:

___ Often.

___ Sometimes.

___ Rarely.

___ Never.

___ N/A.

I generally:

___ Bite off more than I can chew.

___ Am a good judge of taking on what I can accomplish.

___ Avoid taking on any additional tasks because I fear becoming too busy.

Regarding distractions: (check all that apply)

___ If people drop into my office or cubicle to chat, I usually talk with them even if I'm busy.

___ If people drop into my office or cubicle to chat, I'm good at keeping it brief if I am busy.

___ I always answer my desk phone or cell phone when it rings.

___ I check who's calling, then only answer if necessary or convenient.

___ I often welcome distractions because I'm avoiding what I should be doing.

___ Distractions are a real problem for my productivity.

___ Distractions are somewhat of a problem for my productivity.

___ Distractions aren't a problem for me.

Regarding working on specific tasks: (check all that apply)

___ I avoid tasks I don't like.

___ I avoid tasks my boss assigns that I think are stupid or irrelevant.

___ I avoid getting started on big projects.

___ I can have a hard time getting started on things even when I enjoy them.

___ I save the tasks I like the least for last.

___ Other: _____.

Regarding work-related phone calls:

___ I return most work-related phone calls within 24 hours.

___ I eventually return most work-related phone calls.

___ I rarely return work-related phone calls.

Regarding reading email:

___ I read my email as soon as it lands in my inbox; it is a job requirement.

___ I read my email as soon as it lands in my inbox; it's not a job requirement and it interferes with my work.

___ I read my email as soon as it lands in my inbox; it's not a job requirement and it's not a problem for me.

___ I check my email a lot; it interferes with my work.

___ I check my email a lot; it isn't a problem for my productivity.

___ I check my email at a few prescribed times during the day.

Regarding work-related emails:

___ I return most work-related emails as soon as I read them.

___ I return most work-related emails within 24 hours.

___ I rarely return work-related emails.

Regarding personal emails that arrive during work time:

___ They are significantly interfering with my work productivity.

___ They are somewhat interfering with my work productivity.

___ They are not interfering with my work productivity.

___ I don't read them at work.

Regarding work-related paperwork:

___ I keep up pretty well with work-related paperwork.

___ I'm usually a little behind in work-related paperwork.

___ I'm usually fairly behind in work-related paperwork.

___ I'm so behind I don't even know where to start.

Regarding getting to meetings and appointments, I usually get there:

___ Before they start.

___ Just as they start.

___ Up to 5 minutes after they start.

___ More than 5 minutes after they start.

I feel most energetic and productive: (check all that apply)

___ Early morning.

___ Mid- to late morning.

___ Right after lunch.

___ Mid- to late afternoon.

___ Right after dinner.

___ Late at night.

___ Rarely or never.

If you think you waste too much time at work, what are the biggest problems for you? (Select as many as apply, but rank in order: 1= worst problem, 2= second worst problem, etc.)

___ Distracted by internet (personal email, social networking, web-surfing, online games, etc.)

___ Distracted by co-workers

___ Difficulty sitting still; I'm always finding reasons to get up and move around.

___ Distracted by cell phone, texting, etc.

___ Find myself daydreaming, or have a hard time focusing

___ Dislike a lot of the tasks I have to do

___ Other: _____

I feel like work intrudes on my personal life:

___ Often, but that's fine with me.

___ Often; I don't like it.

___ Occasionally.

___ Rarely.

Overall, on a scale of 1-10 where
1 = "I use my time at work very productively," and
10 = "I use my time at work very poorly,"

I would give myself a rating of: _____.

What priority level would you give to making changes to your professional time management?

___ High priority   ___ Medium priority   ___ Low priority

Your Professional Stuff and Space

Did you know that a University of Texas study[1] found that people with messy offices are less efficient, less organized and less creative than people with clean offices? Even if that's not true for you, the study also found that people with messy offices are *perceived* to be inefficient and unimaginative!

As I answer this questionnaire, I am describing my:

___ Home office

___ Space at work

Rate the following according to this scale:

    1 = Usually neat, clean and well organized
    2 = A bit cluttered, but I can usually find things pretty easily
    3 = Medium cluttered; could definitely use some help
    4 = Pretty messy; finding things is pretty difficult
    5 = In danger of being declared a federal disaster area

	1	2	3	4	5	N/A
Overall appearance of office						
Desk top						
Other horizontal surfaces						
Desk drawers						
File drawers						
Bookcase						
Computer files						
Computer desktop						
Briefcase						
Other:						

How long would it take you to find:	Under 10 Seconds	Probably a Minute or Two	It Would Take a While	N/A
A stapler				
Your employment contract/documents				
A working blue or black pen				
A red pen				
A paper clip				
A flash drive (aka thumb drive)				
A sharp pencil (or mechanical one that's not empty)				
A current paper or electronic memo you need to look at				
A pair of scissors				
Other:				

When it comes to putting away the stuff in my office:

____ Everything has a place.

____ Most things have a place.

____ There's a fair amount that sits out because it doesn't have a place.

____ There's a large amount that sits out because it doesn't have a place.

The main reason that things in my office don't have a place is because:

____ I don't have enough space.

____ I have enough space; I just never got around to assigning them a place.

____ N/A; most things in my office have a place.

Do you use the top of your desk for storage (not counting a few frequently-used items like a pen/pencil holder, paperclip holder, etc.)?

___ I haven't seen the top of my desk in years.

___ Yes, a fair amount.

___ A little.

___ I don't store anything on the top of my desk.

What percentage of the top of your desk can you see when you walk into the office most mornings?

___ 75-100%

___ 50-75%

___ 25-50%

___ 0-25%

Overall, on a scale of 1-10 where
1 = "My professional stuff and space are completely under control," and
10 = "My professional stuff and space are completely out of control,"

I would give myself a rating of: _____.

What priority level would you give making changes to your professional stuff and space issues?

___ High priority   ___ Medium priority   ___ Low priority

Your Professional Information Management

I work:

___ For myself.

___ For an employer.

I have the following piles in my work space awaiting my attention: (check all that apply)

___ Magazines and other professional reading

___ Non-junk mail that I'm going to get to eventually

___ Junk mail and catalogs I want to go through

___ Memos that are current

___ Memos that are probably out of date

___ Paper that needs to be filed, recycled or otherwise dealt with

___ Items that have been there for ages

___ Stuff that should be tossed, like old drink cups and other disposables

___ Items that I'm currently working on

___ Other: _____

The business cards that people give me are:

___ All over the place.

___ In one specific place, but not sorted.

___ Sorted and filed or scanned into the computer.

___ Other: _____

The computer that I use at work is: (check all that apply)

___ A laptop.

___ A desktop.

___ Owned by me.

___ Owned by my company.

The information I keep on my work computer is:

___ Work-related only.

___ Work-related and personal.

The information I have on my computer is:

___ Extremely important.

___ Pretty important.

___ Somewhat important.

___ Not at all important.

The data on my work computer is backed up:

___ Daily or more often.

___ Once a week.

___ At least once a month.

___ Never.

___ Not sure; the company takes care of it.

When a brilliant idea strikes me, I:

___ Write it down so I don't forget it, but I usually can't find it later.

___ Write it down so I don't forget it; I know exactly where it is.

___ Usually remember it without writing it down.

___ Usually try to remember it but usually forget it.

When I go to a class, meeting or conference, I usually:

___ Take a bunch of handouts but never look at them.

___ Take a bunch of handouts, look over them and discard the ones I don't want.

___ Take a bunch of handouts and read them all.

___ Take a few handouts and read the ones that I take.

___ Take a few handouts but usually don't get to them.

How much junk mail do you get at work?

___ I don't get much junk mail.

___ I get a lot of junk mail.

What do you do with junk mail that comes to your office?

___ Save most of it to look at sometime but never get to it

___ Recycle most of it immediately

___ Read what is useful in a timely fashion and recycle the rest

___ Other: _____

Which most closely describes your professional magazine, newspaper and other *non-electronic* subscriptions?

___ I'm generally caught up on my reading.

___ I'm a bit behind on my reading.

___ I'm hopelessly behind on my reading.

___ I don't have any non-electronic subscriptions.

When I'm finished with a magazine or other periodical, I:

___ Put it in a pile with other old periodicals.

___ Recycle the whole thing.

___ Cut out and file or scan anything I'll want to refer to and recycle the rest.

___ Cut out anything I want to refer to and stick it on a pile somewhere, then recycle the rest.

___ Rarely get around to finishing magazines, so they stack up.

___ Other: _____.

Which most closely describes your professional *electronic* subscriptions?

___ I'm generally caught up on my reading.

___ I'm a bit behind on my reading.

___ I'm hopelessly behind on my reading.

___ I don't have any electronic subscriptions.

My professional file drawers are: (check all that apply)

___ Mostly organized.

___ Mostly disorganized.

___ Full of stuff that I'll probably never need again.

___ Filled with files I might need but rarely use that are taking up prime filing space instead of being archived elsewhere.

___ A total disaster.

___ Not full and have space for additional filing.

___ Jammed full.

Regarding email: (check all that apply)

___ I read every email that comes into my email box, including junk mail, jokes, spam, etc.

___ I usually quickly delete spam, jokes, etc. without reading.

___ I have a good spam filter.

___ I spend about the right amount of time on my email.

___ I spend too much time on my email.

___ My email time is way out of control.

Overall, on a scale of 1-10 where
1 = "My professional information is completely under control," and
10 = "My professional information is completely out of control,"

I would give myself a rating of: _____.

What priority level would you give to making changes to your professional information management?

___ High priority   ___ Medium priority   ___ Low priority

Endnotes

Tool #8: *Reward Yourself*

[1] Jon E. Roeckelein (1998), *Dictionary of Theories, Laws, and Concepts in Psychology*, Greenwood, ISBN 0-313-30460-2 p. 384.

Tool #10: Get Support

[1] Gollwitzer, Peter M., Paschal Sheeran, Verena Michalski, and Andrea E. Seifert. 'When Intentions Go Public: Does Social Reality Widen the Intention-Behavior Gap?' *Psychological Science* 20.5 (2009): 612-18. Print.

Overcoming Obstacles

[1] Prochaska, James O., John C. Norcross, and Carlo C. DiClemente. *Changing for Good*. New York: Quill, 2002. Print.

[2] Smith, Manuel J. *When I Say No, I Feel Guilty*. New York, NY: Bantam, 1975. Print.

[3] Roggli, Linda, and Wendy Sefcik. *Confessions of an ADDiva: Midlife in the Non-linear Lane*. Durham, NC: Passionate Possibility, 2011. Print.

Appendix – *Your Professional Stuff and Space*

[1] Gosling, Samuel D., Sei Jin Ko, Thomas Mannarelli, and Margaret E. Morris. "A Room With A Cue: Personality Judgments Based On Offices And Bedrooms." *Journal of Personality and Social Psychology* 82.3 (2002): 379-398. Print.